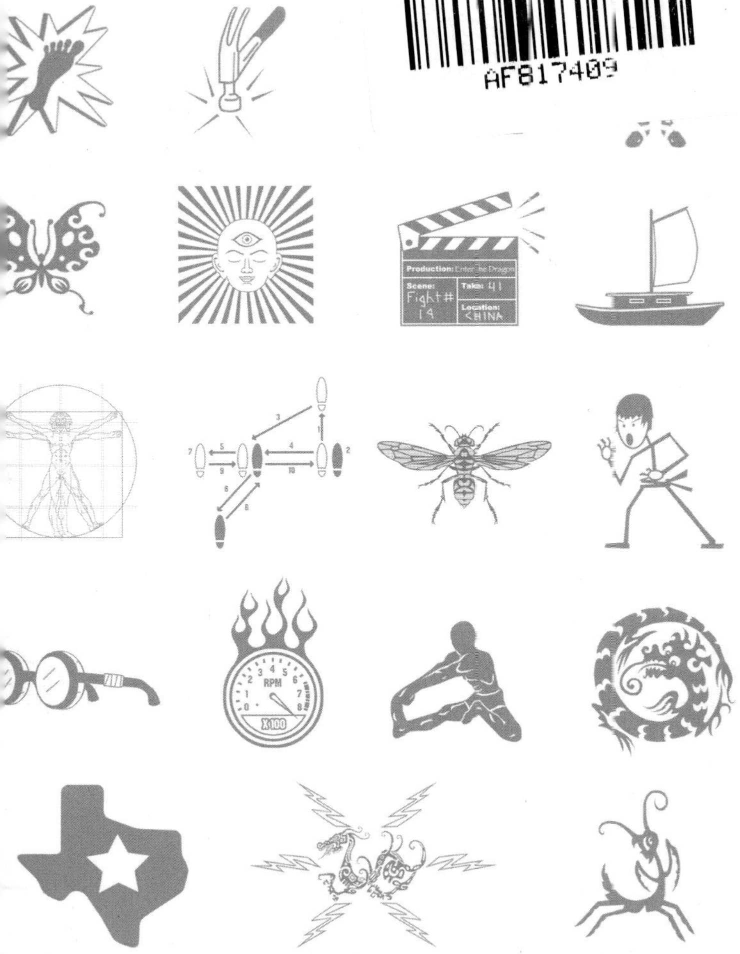
Production: Enter the Dragon
Scene: Fight # 14
Take: 41
Location: CHINA
RPM
X100

POISED to PUMMEL

POISED to PUMMEL

an unauthorized biography of Bruce Lee

illustrator
Aaron Block

biographer
John Marcoux

Ki-YAH
John Marcoux

Dinner Guest Press

Bite-Size Bios
since
2011

Published by Dinner Guest Press
An illinois limited liability corporation

Library of Congress Cataloging-in-Publication Data

Block, Aaron
Marcoux, John.
poised to pummel:
an unauthorized biography of bruce lee / Aaron Block and John Marcoux.
P. cm.
ISBN-978-0-9837813-0-1

[1.
] I. Title

First Edition November 2011

All quotes attributable to Bruce Lee are typed in
Helvetica Neue, medium condensed oblique.
When spoken in first person, no quotation marks are used.

Printed in China

Book Layout:

Eric Lower - e@ericlower.com

In memory of
two who knew kung fu

Al Miller + Matt Adler

Bruce Lee is welcome to our dinner table anytime.
His on-screen awesomeness, by itself, justifies the invite. But if you read about this man's life, you'll discover more reasons to dine with him. He persisted along a heroic path that evoked his greatest character, or, as this biography posits, an entire cast of great characters. From young punk to peerless master, Bruce Lee radiated transcendent skill into his thirty-second year, just long enough to achieve his goal and make the "f#@%ingest" action movie ever.

We aim for accuracy.
We surveyed his life, meditated on his evolution, and identified a few dozen real-life roles he fulfilled on his way towards immortality. Find the scholarship behind each layout in the Bibliography and Source Notes at the end of the book. Please email eat@BiteSizeBios.com with corrections.

We illustrate to help you cogitate.
The accompanying illustrations emphasize, amplify, teach, symbolize, report, comment, criticize, illuminate, satirize, and dramatically re-enact the biographical facts and quotes selected and arranged in each character layout. We avoided the merely literal and conventional depictions that fans might find on posters and t-shirts (think, for example, of that iconic image of a provoked Bruce Lee, shirtless and sporting freshly-inflicted razor slices across his abdomen). We respect Bruce Lee's post-mortem intellectual property rights of publicity because it is the right thing to do and because he could still kick our asses.

to

Howard Stern

champion of free expression and a
man who prefers books with lots of pictures.

www.BiteSizeBios.com

CHARACTERS

- Punk
- Seeker
- Student
- Struggler
- Visionary
- Perfectionist
- Defender
- Anticipator
- Kicker
- Puncher
- Jogger
- Dancer
- Rhythmist
- Exploder
- Psychologist
- Philosopher
- Iconoclast
- Economist
- Improviser
- Sufferer
- Author
- Entertainer
- TV Star
- Movie Star
- Choreographer
- Speedster
- Real Deal
- Alpha Male
- Cruiser
- Yogi
- Stoner
- Endurer
- Mortal
- Hero
- Superstar
- Anatomy

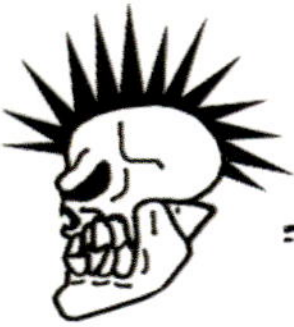

Punk

PUNK

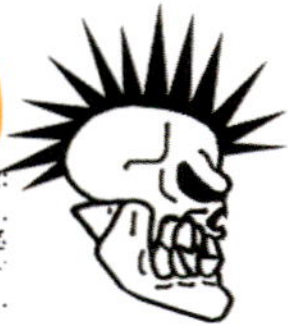

The Fury Came First.

As a kid in Hong Kong, I was a punk and went looking for fights.

I was extremely mischievous, aggressive, hot-tempered, and fierce.

We used chains and pens with knives hidden inside.

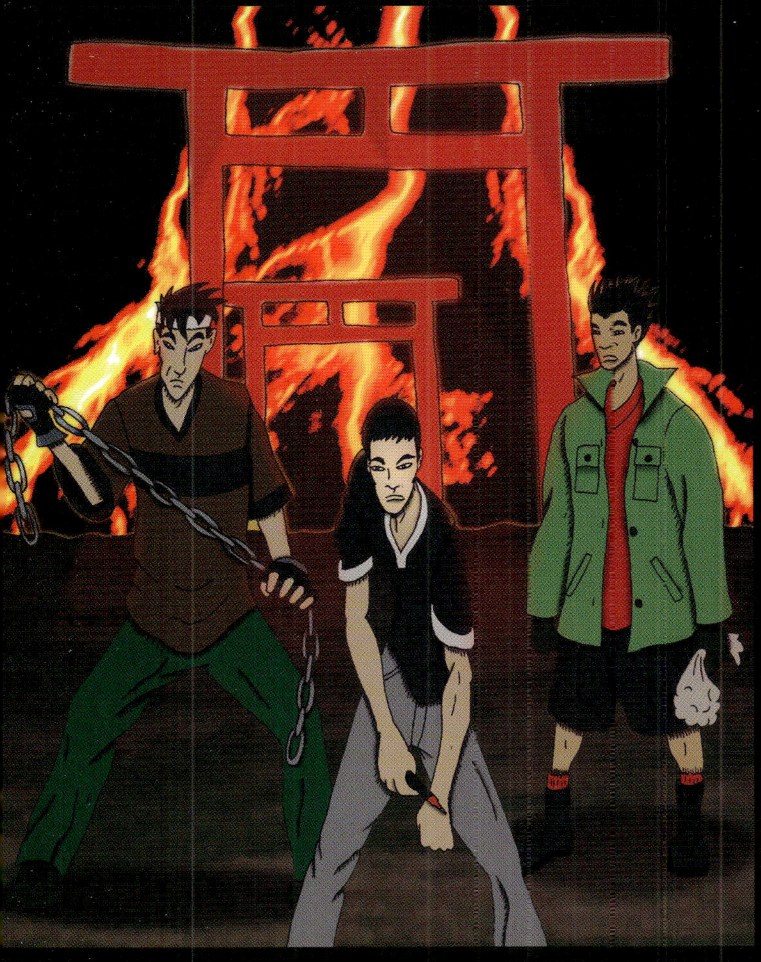

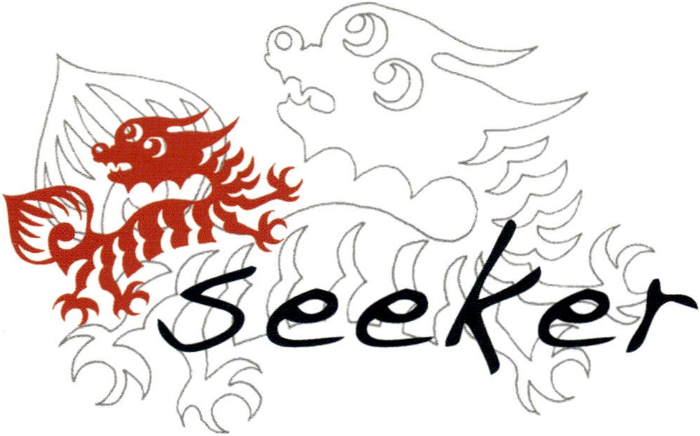

Bruce sought skill because
he ***despised*** losing.

I wondered what would happen to me if I didn't have my gang behind me if I got into a fight. I decided to learn how to protect myself.

The young teen found his way
into his first kung fu class.

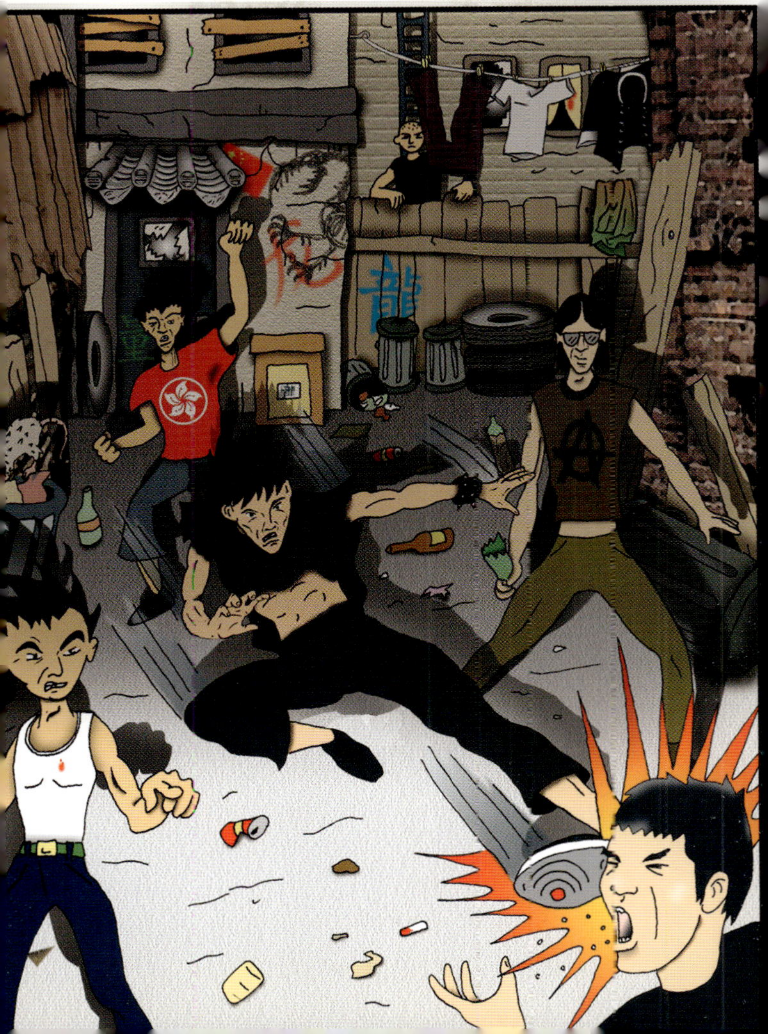
龍

STUDENT

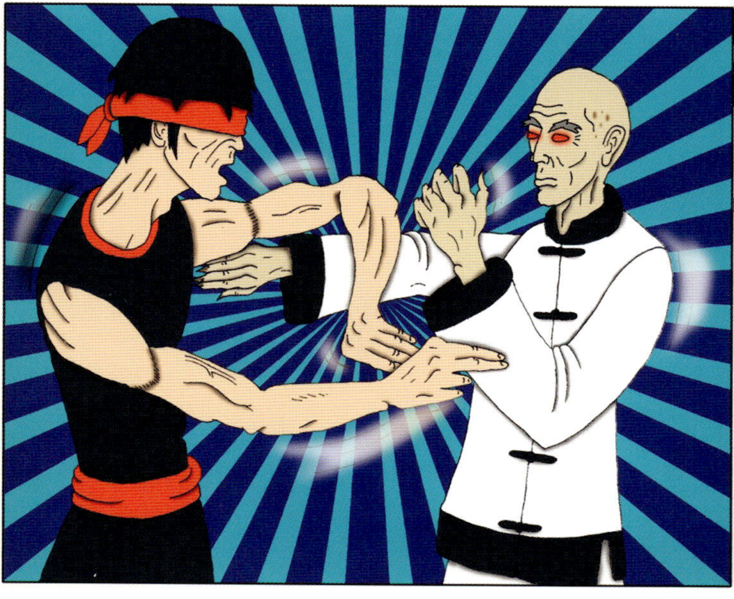

Bruce and his master practiced *sticking hands,* arm fencing that develops a Jedi-like reflex.

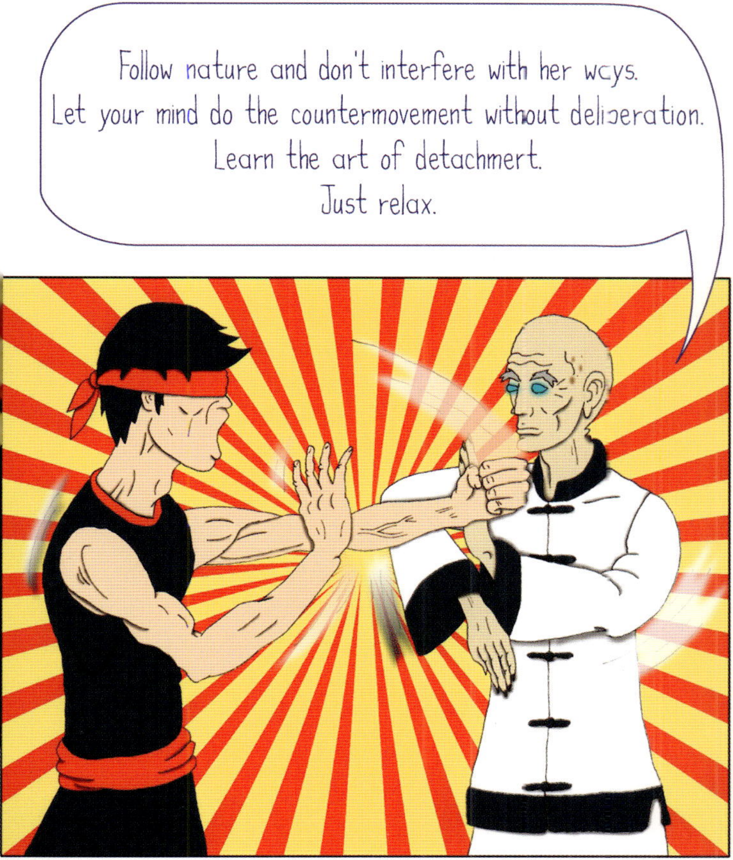

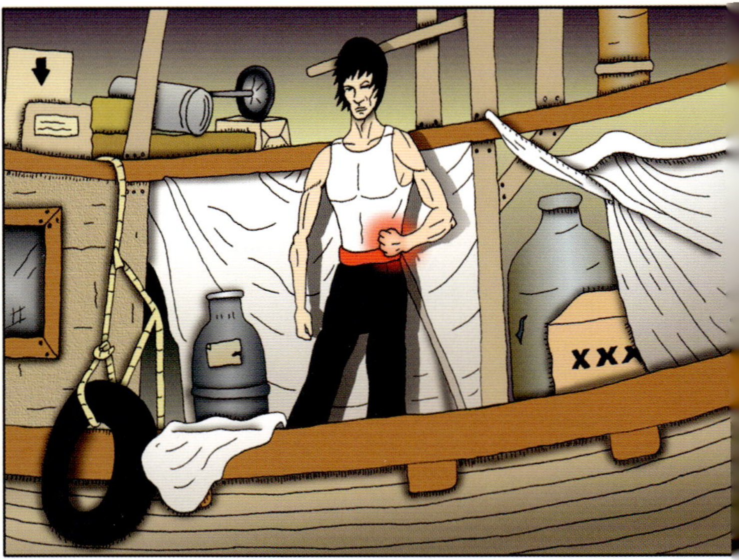

struggler

His intensity sparked rapid improvement, but it also stranded him on a frustrating plateau. He took a boat ride to clear his mind.

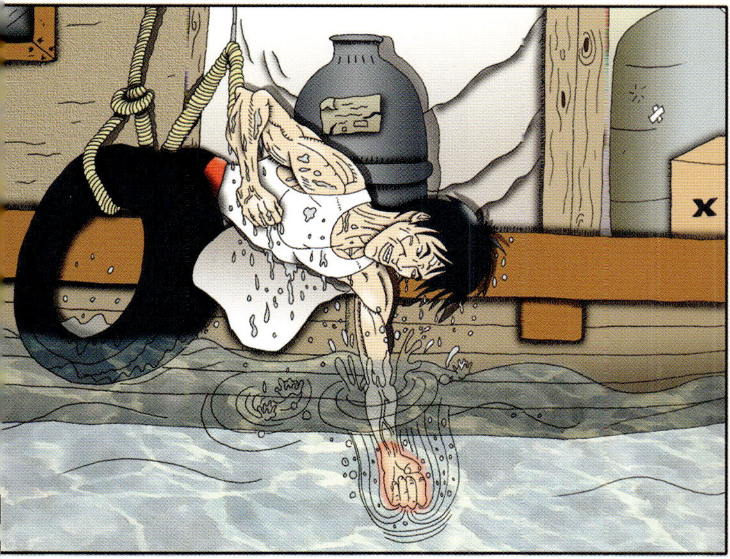

Instead of relaxing,
Bruce raged,
punched the sea,
and experienced an epiphany!

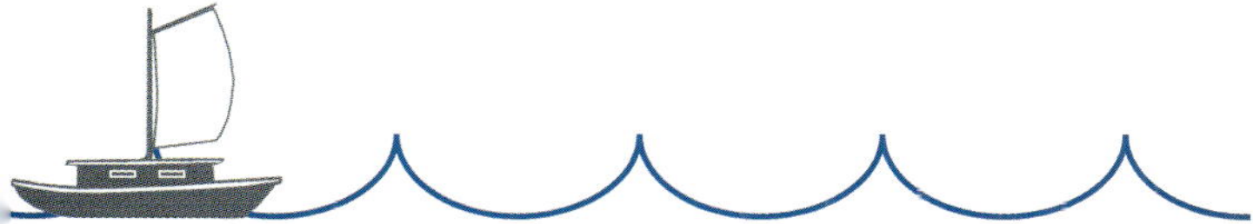

VISIONARY

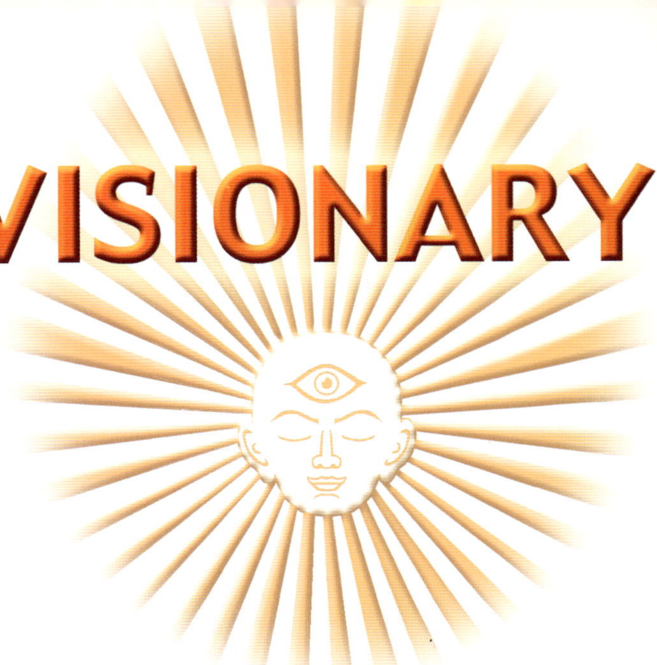

I struck it just now, but it did not suffer hurt. Again I stabbed at it with all my might, yet it was not wounded. I then tried to grasp a handful of it, but it was impossible. Although it seemed weak, it could penetrate the hardest substances in the world.

This is it!

I want to be like the nature of water.

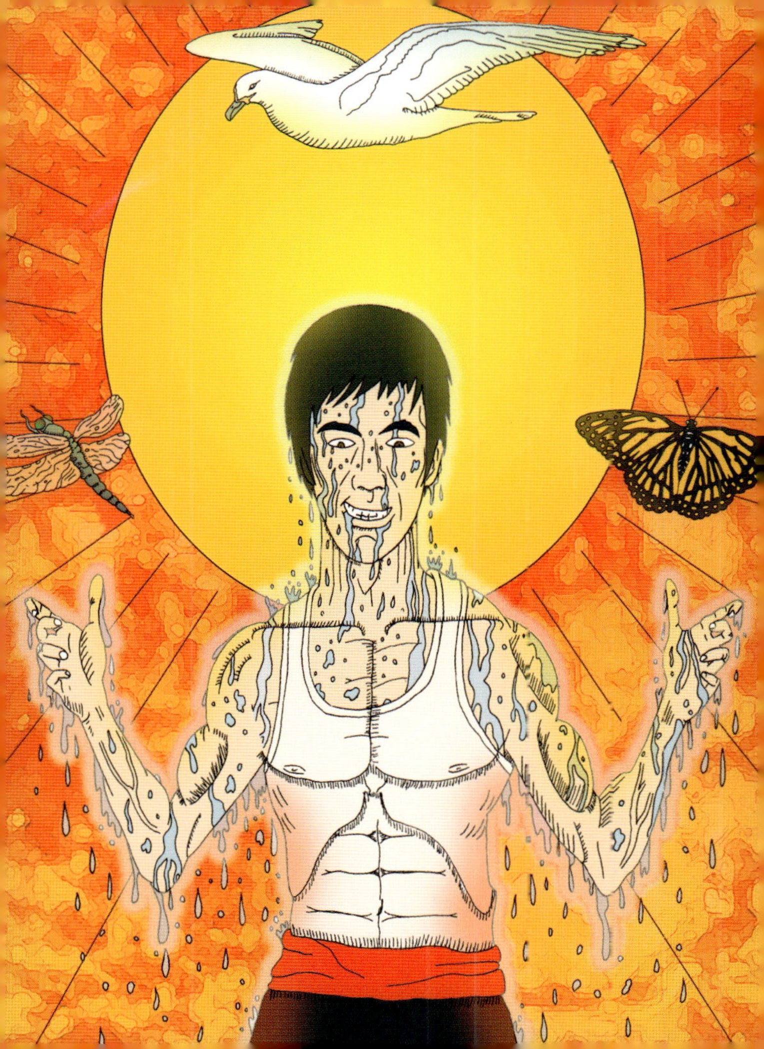

PERFECTIONIST

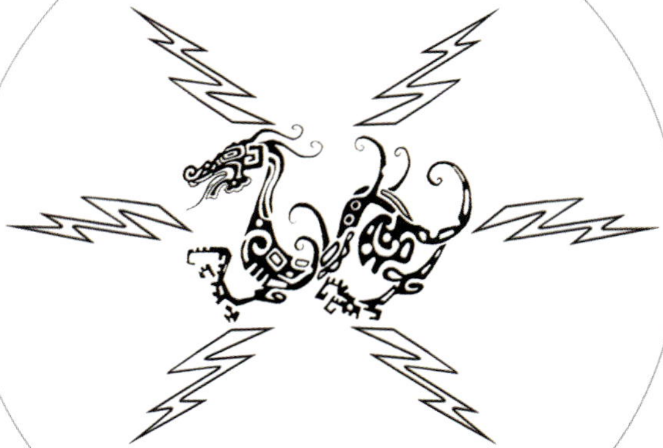

Bruce would repeat, repeat, repeat each move until glowing with precision. He synchronized this physical education with his mental and spiritual evolution.

How can I, in the process of learning how to use my body, come to understand myself?

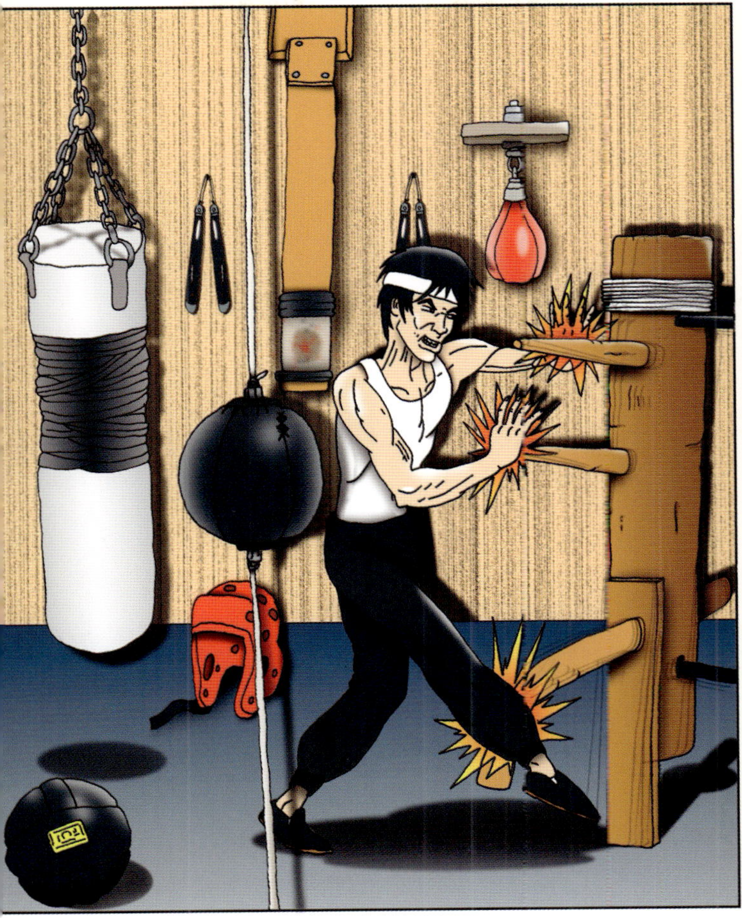

Bruce Lee
preached
self-defense
first.

DEFENDER

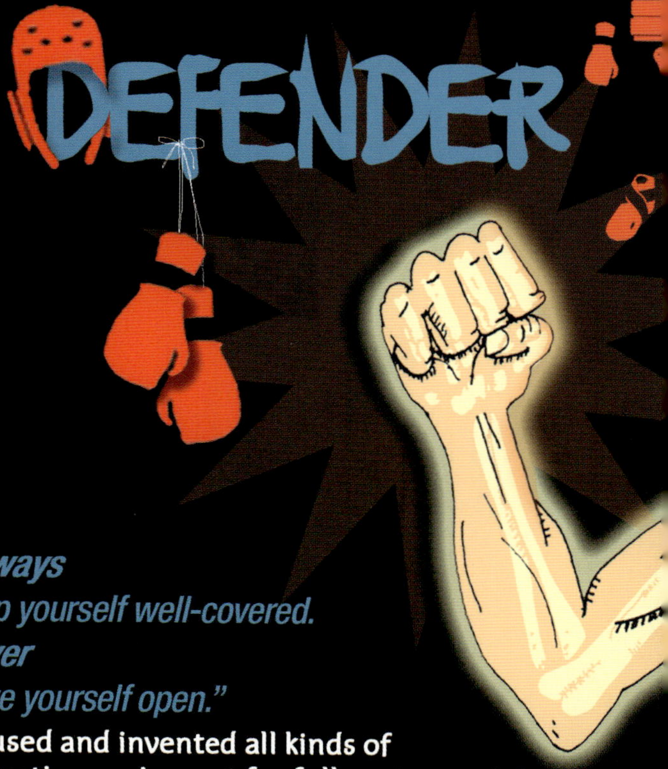

"Always
keep yourself well-covered.
Never
leave yourself open."

He used and invented all kinds of protective equipment for full contact training.

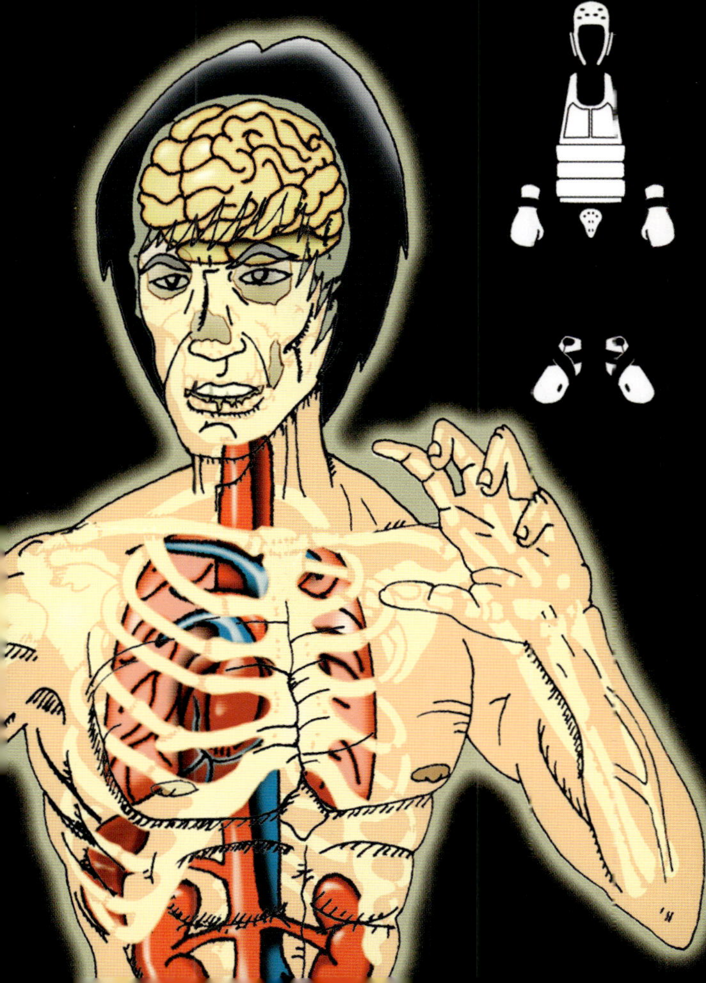

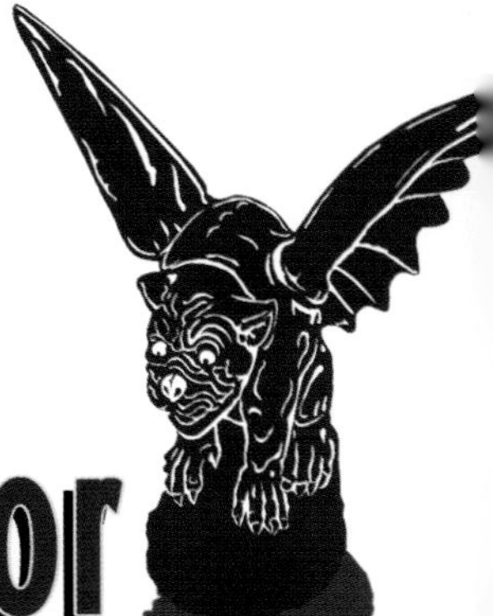

Anticipator

Bruce taught vigilance
to guard against
surprise attacks.

"A good martial artist does not become tense but ready; not thinking yet not dreaming; ready for whatever may come."

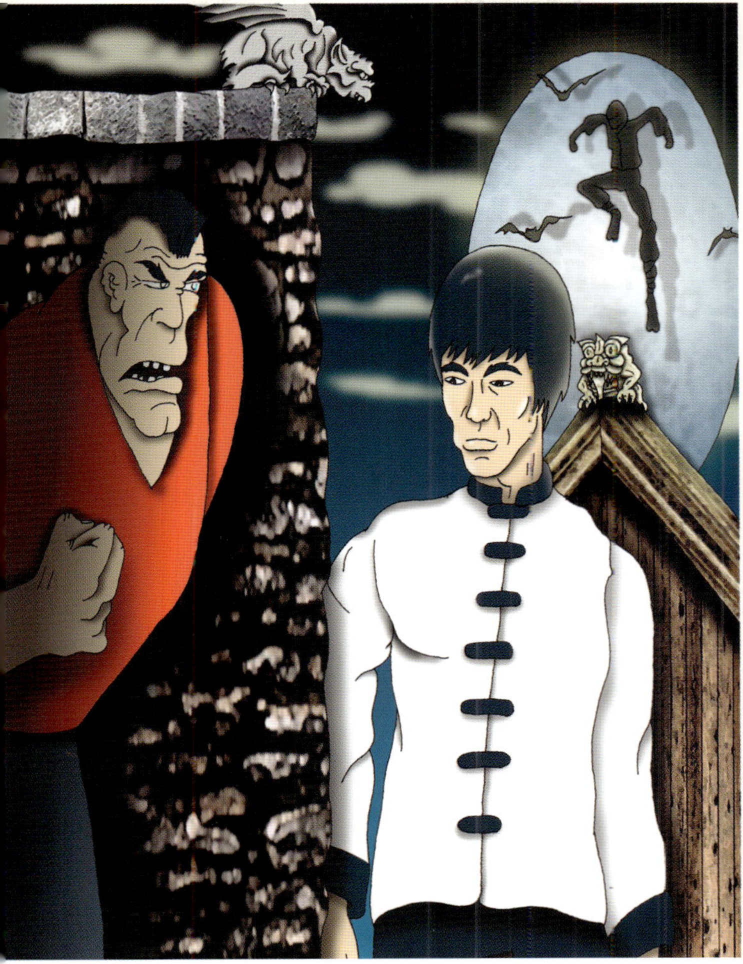

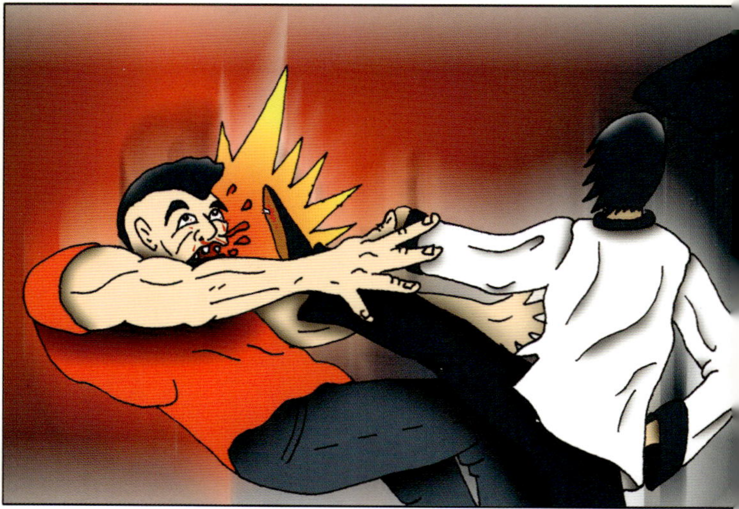

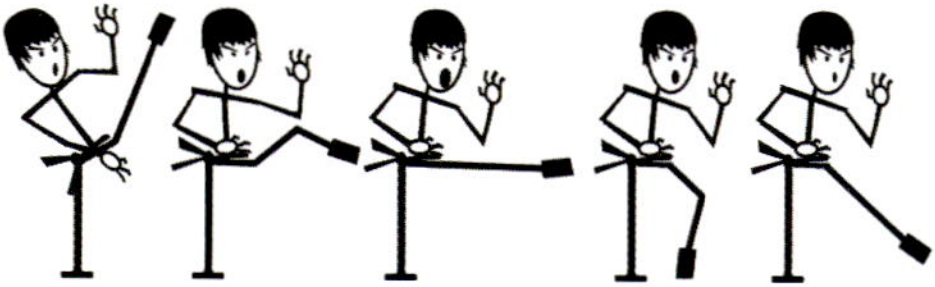

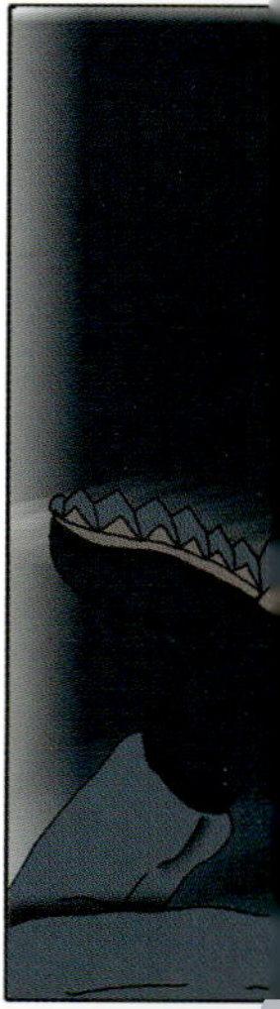

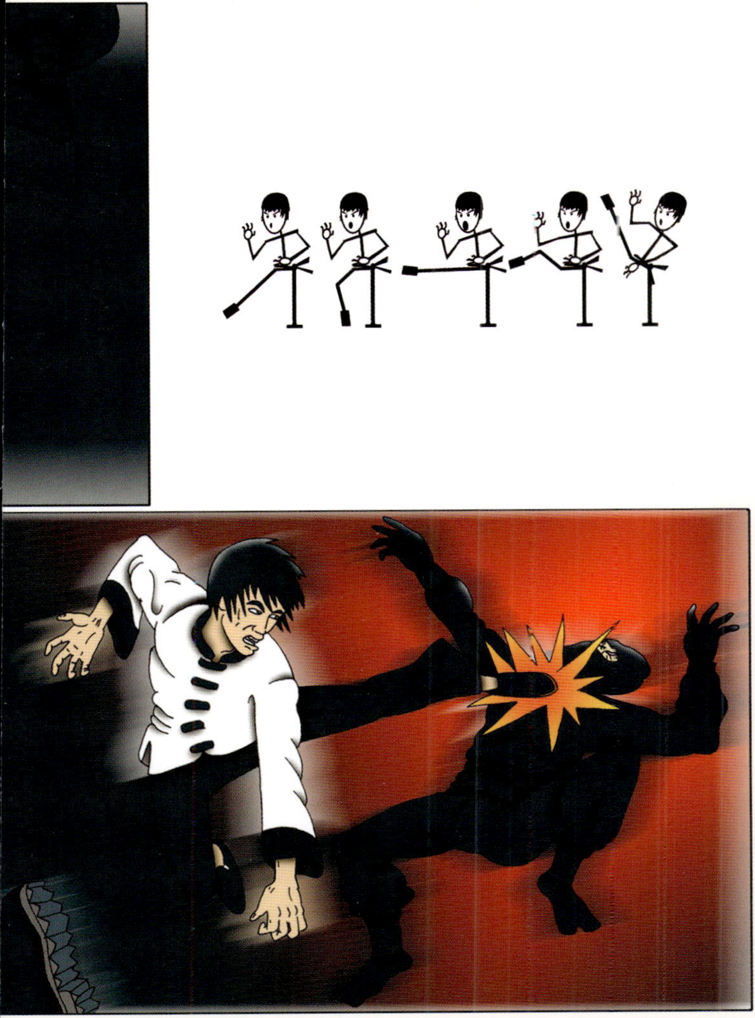

KICKER

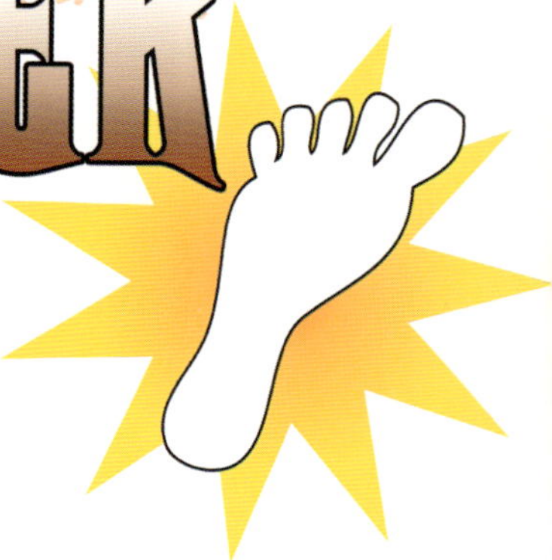

"When you can kick so you aren't jarred but the tree is jarred, then you will begin to understand a kick."

Bruce favored quick strikes with the forward leg because it is one's longest weapon, it wins instantly against a knee or groin, and it transfers *massive* energy.

"It can be compared to your left jab in boxing."

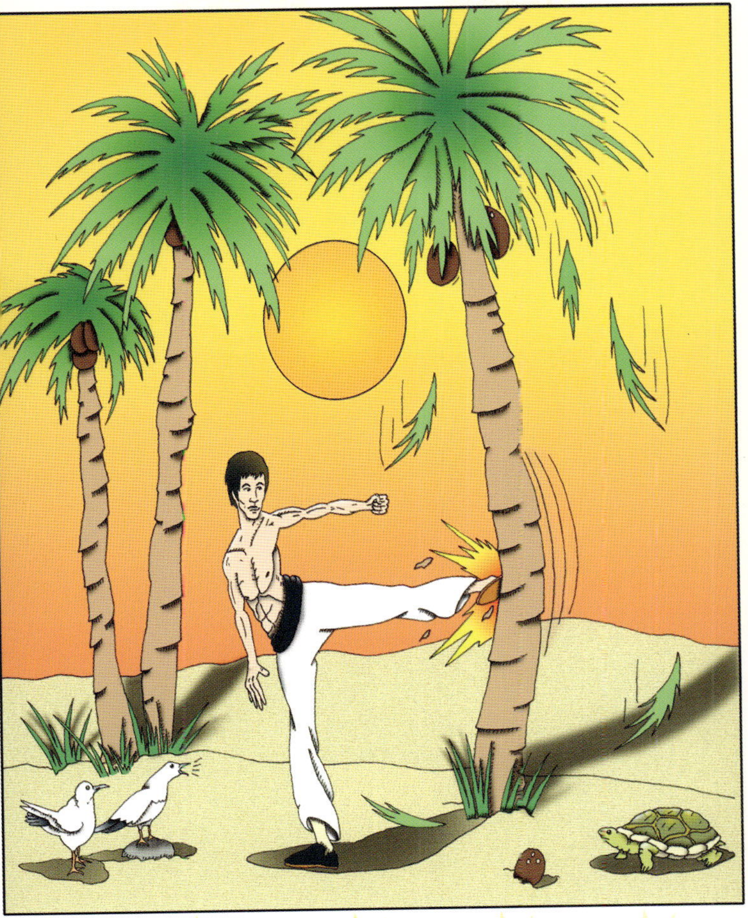

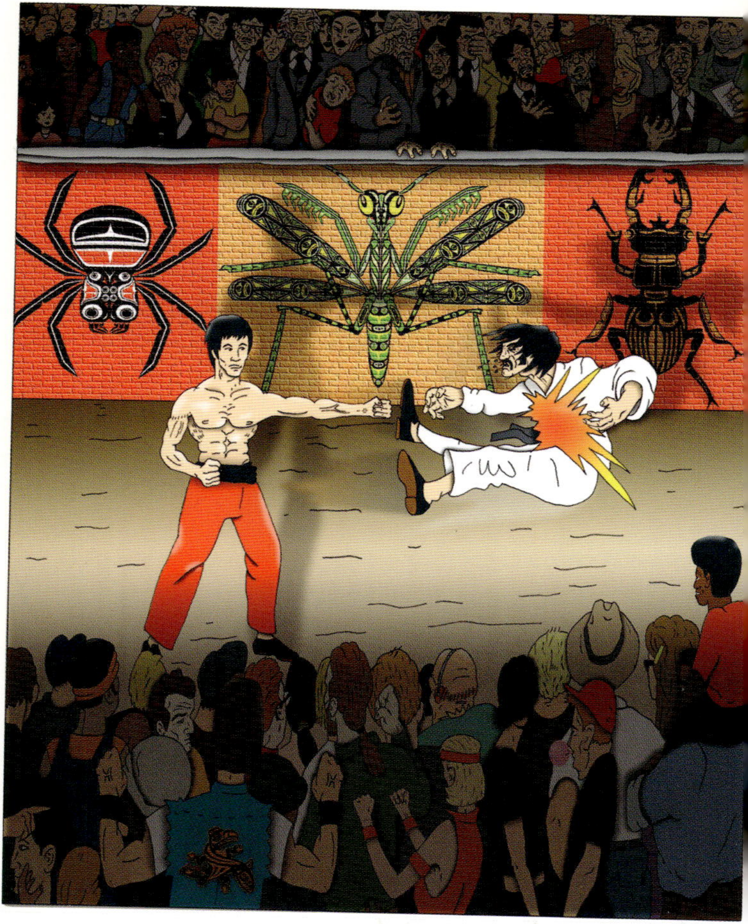

PUNCHER

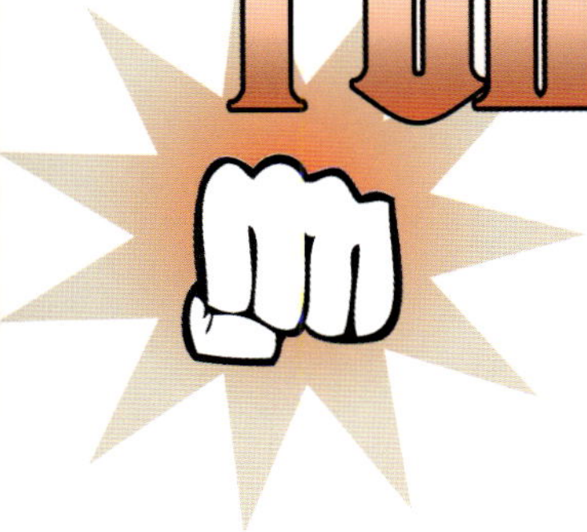

"The power of the punch comes from the correct contact at the right spot and at the right moment with the body in perfect position."

Bruce's superhuman *one-inch punch* earned him an invite to his first Hollywood screen test.

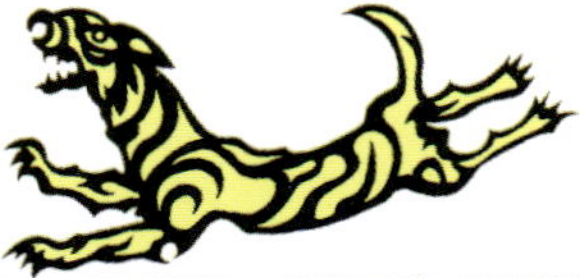

JOGGER

Too winded after beating an inferior opponent, Bruce optimized his fitness. He called jogging *"the king of all exercises"* and a requirement for anyone serious about hard sparring. His dog Bo ran by his side.

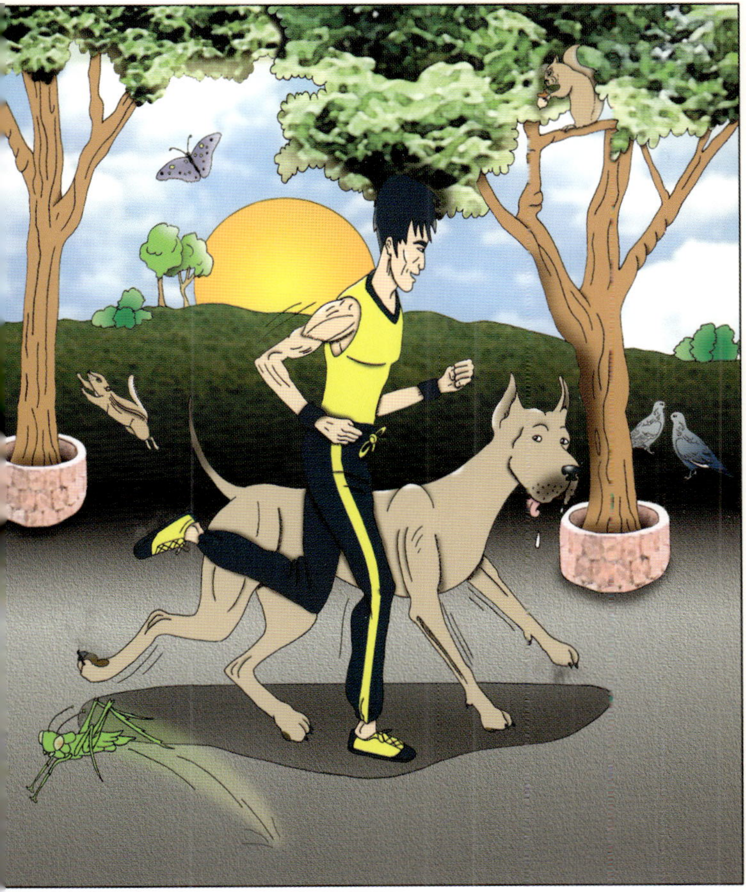

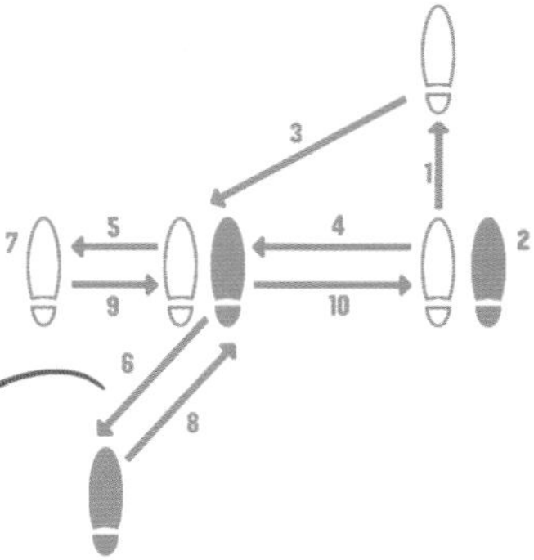

Dancer

His hypnotic agility baffled opponents. Bruce improved footwork through diverse practices including tai chi, skipping rope, boxing, running with leg weights, judo, insect mimicry… he even mastered over 100 cha-cha steps and won a dancing championship.

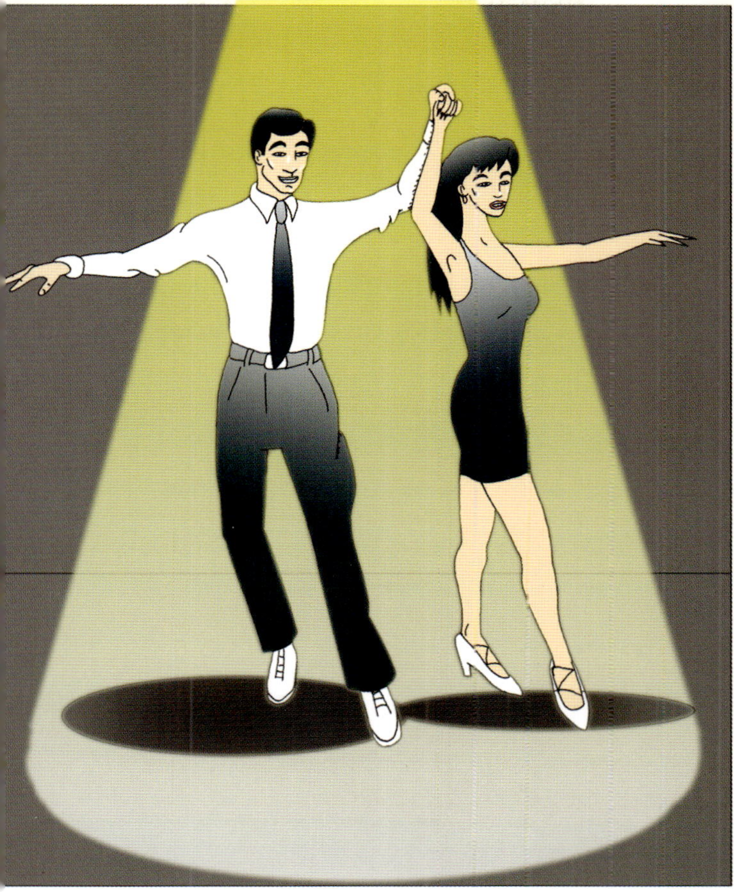

Rhythmist

He studied Indian music and Muhammad Ali for the same reason: to witness the masterful improvisation of rhythm.

Bruce angled his t.v. to face a mirror and mimicked the reverse image of Ali as a southpaw, Bruce's preferred stance.

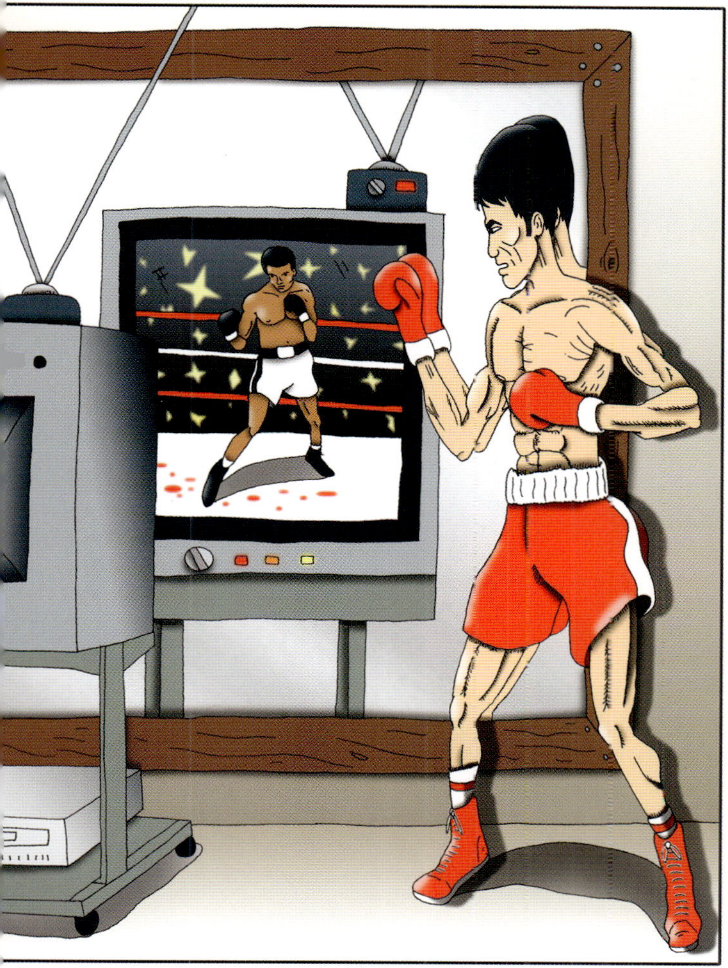

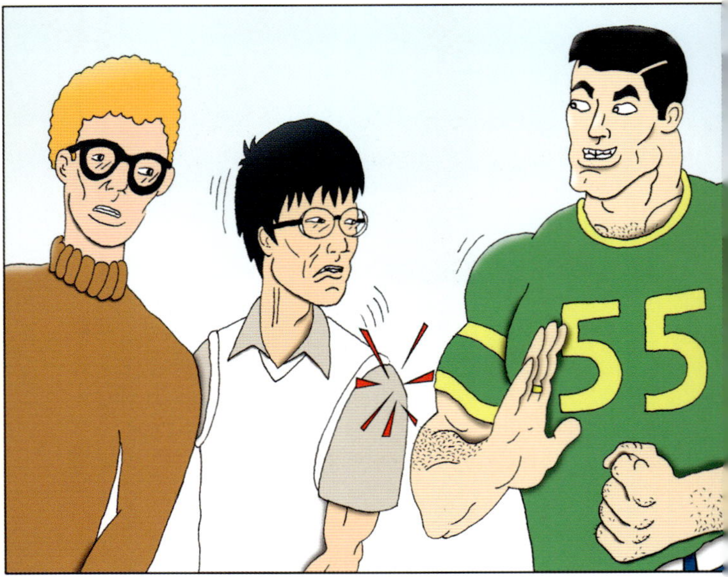

Bruce wore thick glasses to correct his extreme nearsightedness. When an unsuspecting bully mistook the eyewear for weakness, Bruce played along at first, feigning meekness. When the bully attacked, Bruce unleashed...

EXPLODER

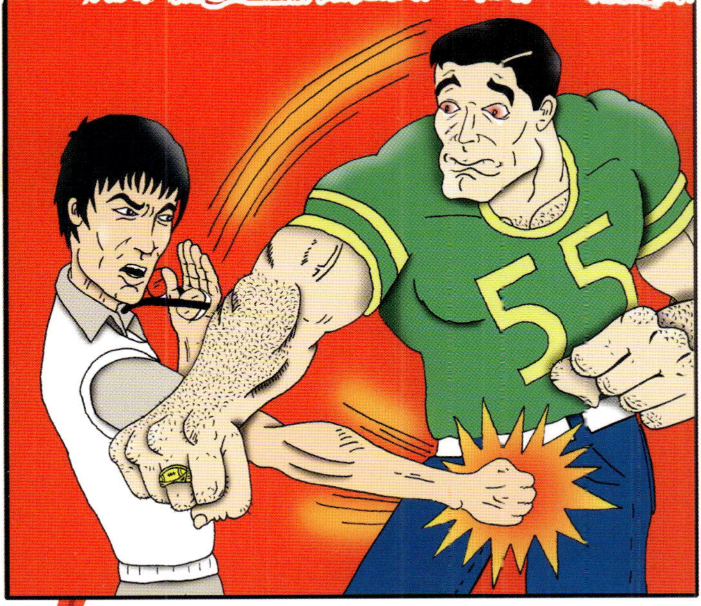

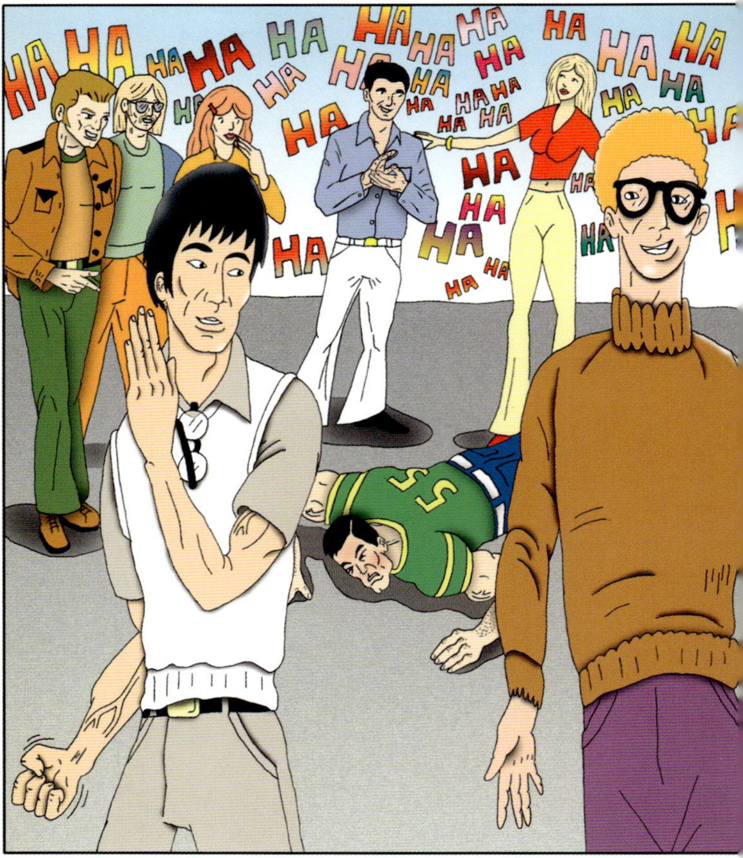

"A person can accept getting beaten by someone who i stronger or bigger than he is... but if he thinks he's bee beaten by a nerd, he'll be pissed off for the rest of his life."

He won with the **body** *and* the **mind.**

Psychologist

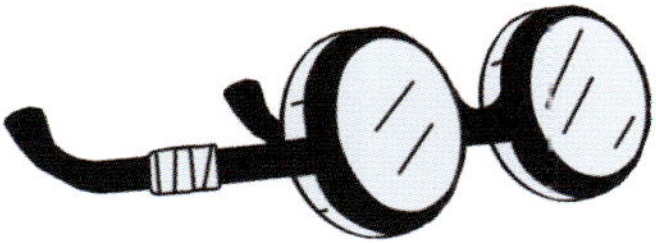

PHILOSOPHER

He illuminated his experience by the light of other great minds, including Jiddu Krishnamurti:

No one can lead another to truth
because truth is infinite
it is a pathless land and
no one can tell you how to find it.

Bruce realized that no martial art system could make a complete fighter because every system has wasteful motions and incomplete arsenals. So he prescribed an anti-system:

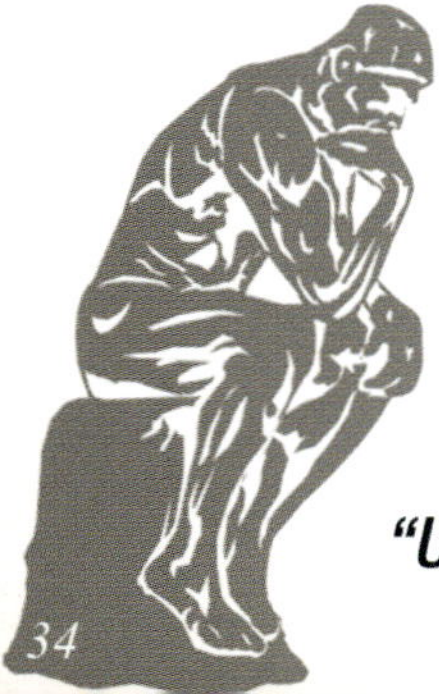

"Use only that which works and take it from any place you can find it."

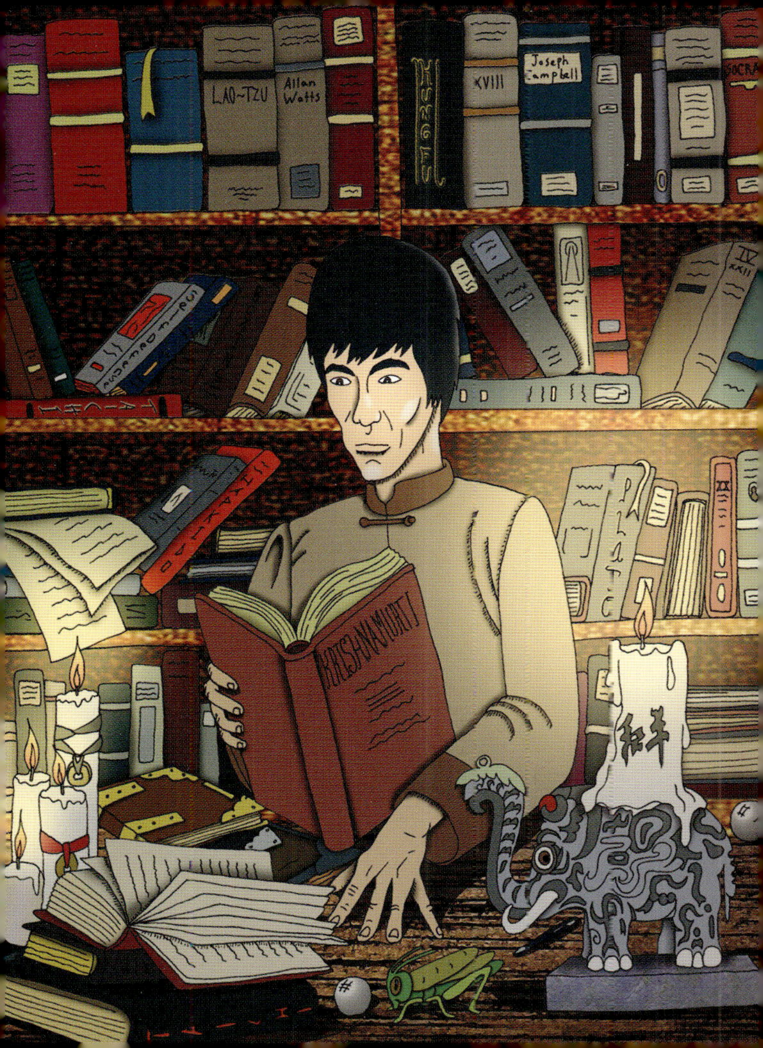
LAO-TZU
Allan Watts
XVIII
Joseph Campbell

ICONOCLAST

Bruce's fight approach smashed the old way of thinking,
what he called ***"the classical mess"*** of traditional martial arts schools
"blindly rehearsing systematic routines and stunts that will lead to nowhere.

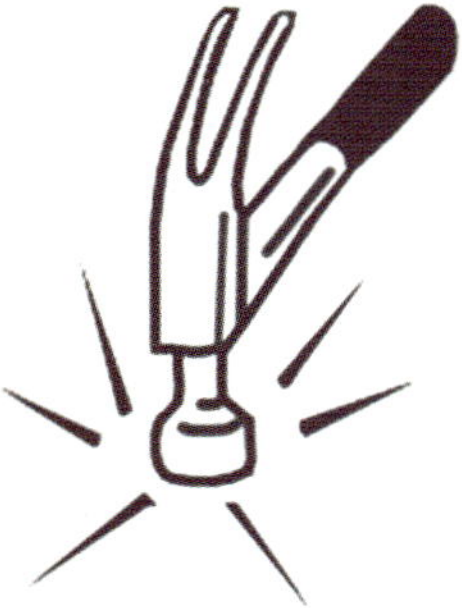

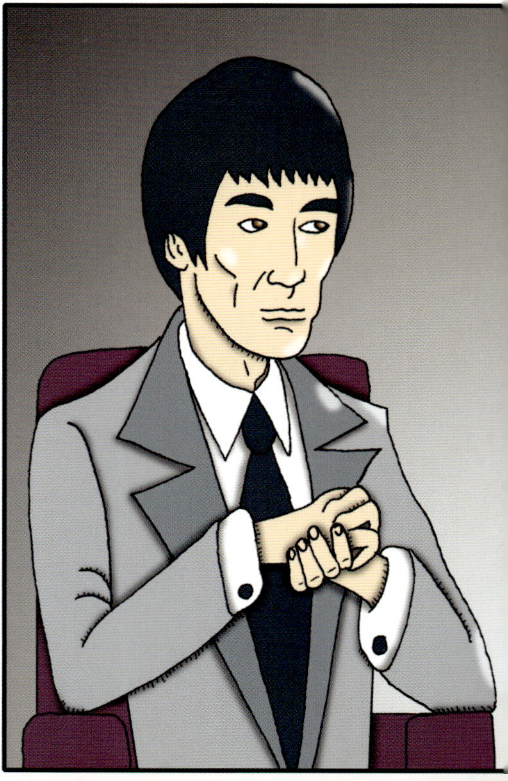

He insisted on realistic training because ***"there is no way a person is going to fight you in the street with a set pattern."*** Bruce challenged all fighters to abandon the fancy baloney and focus on directness.

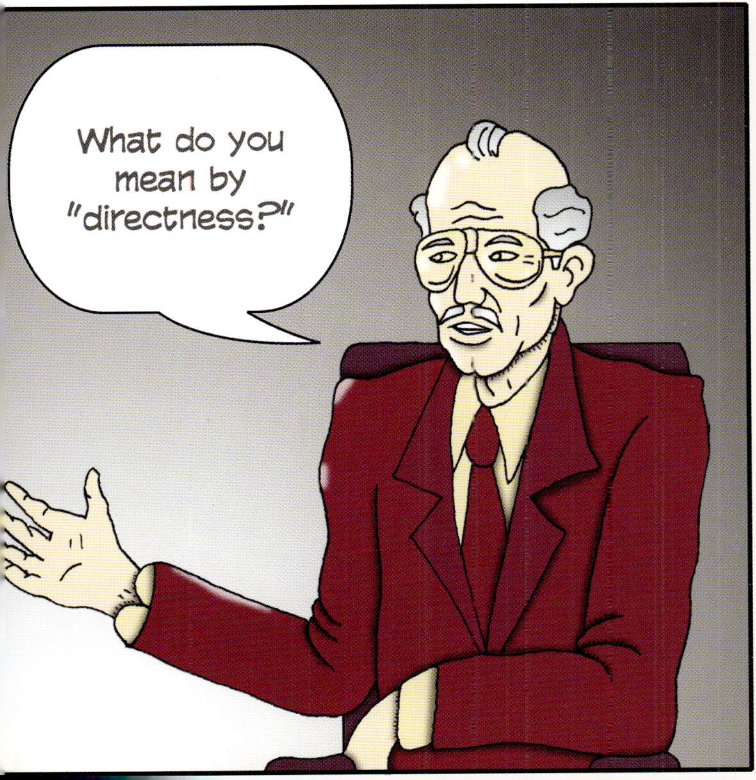

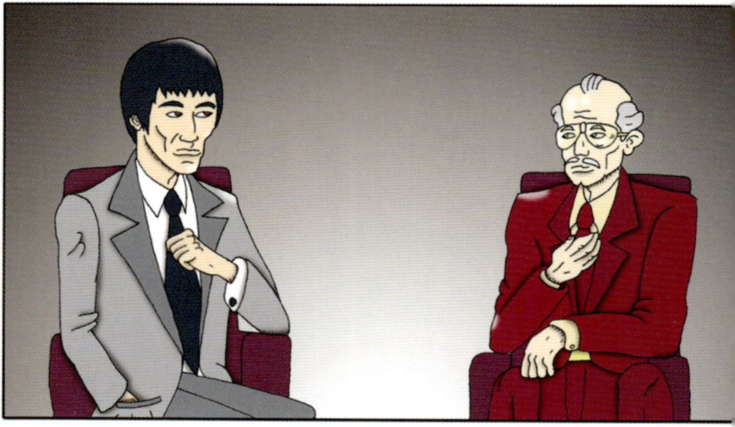

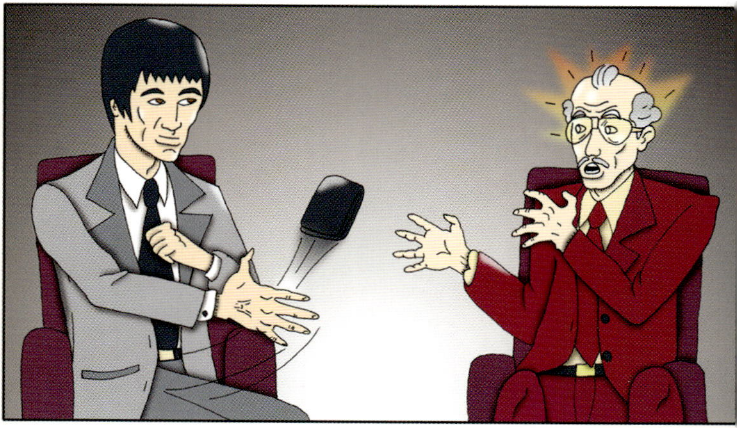

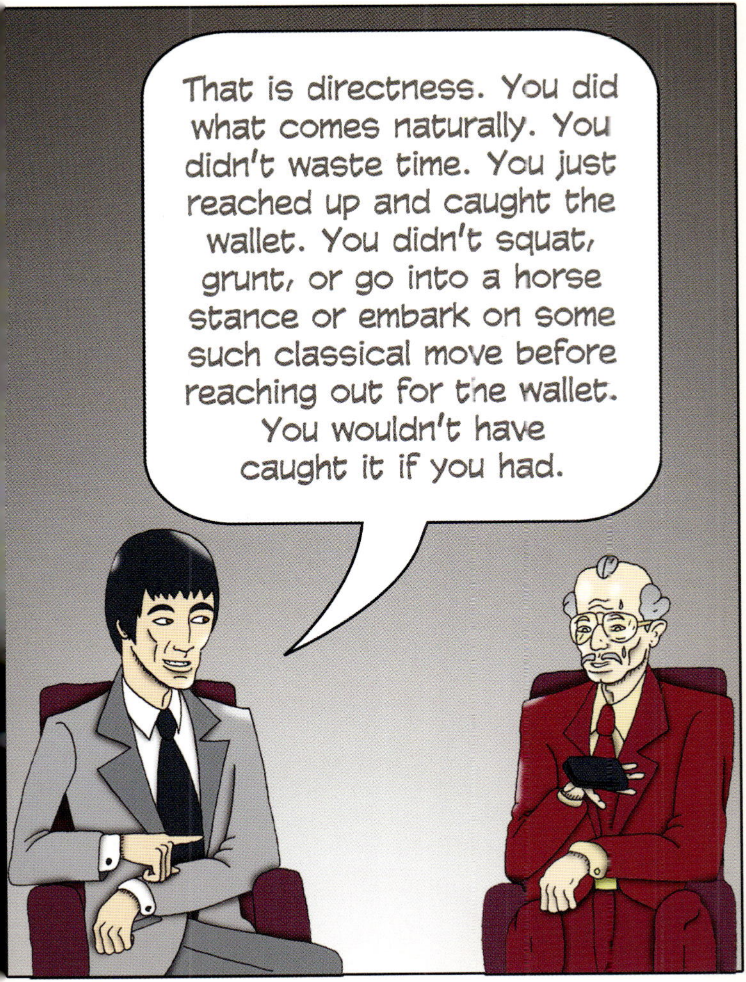
That is directness. You did what comes naturally. You didn't waste time. You just reached up and caught the wallet. You didn't squat, grunt, or go into a horse stance or embark on some such classical move before reaching out for the wallet. You wouldn't have caught it if you had.

economist

Bruce Lee stripped down his techniques for super-efficiency, delivering maximum impact while burning minimal energy.

He marveled at the **stop-hit**, a fencing technique that simultaneously blocks and attacks an opponent. What could be more efficient than deploying a single maneuver that succeeds at both defense and offense?

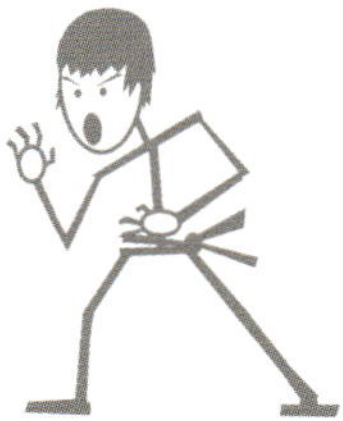

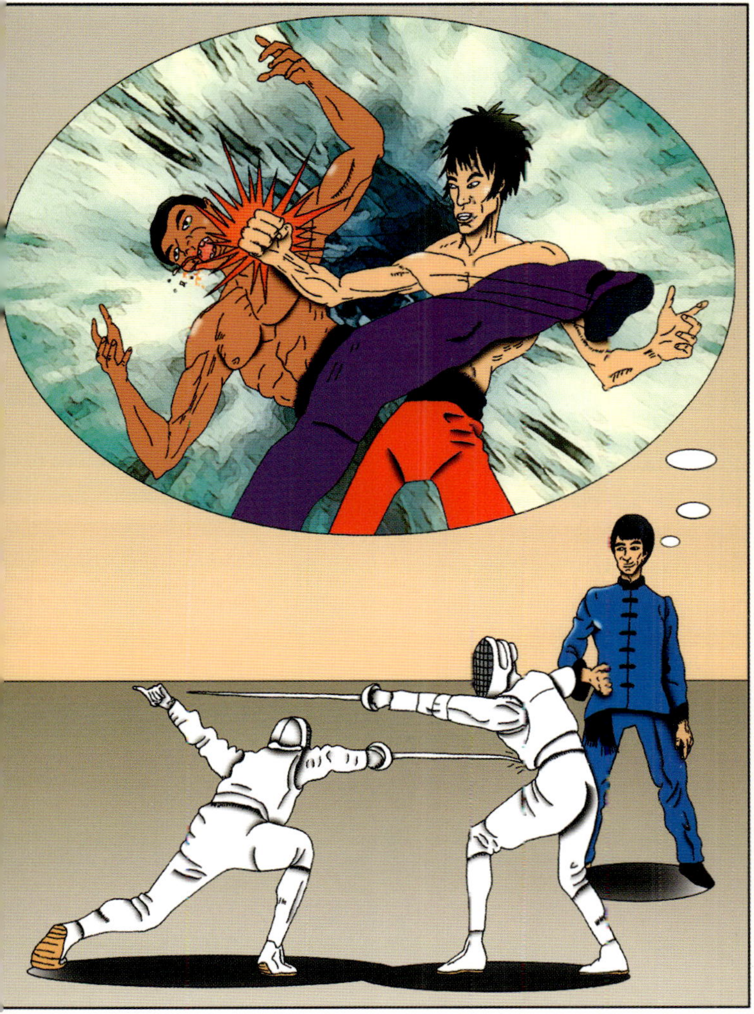

Bruce Lee learned to morph so fluidly in and out of fighting styles that he attained formlessness, the highest level of self-control.

impro

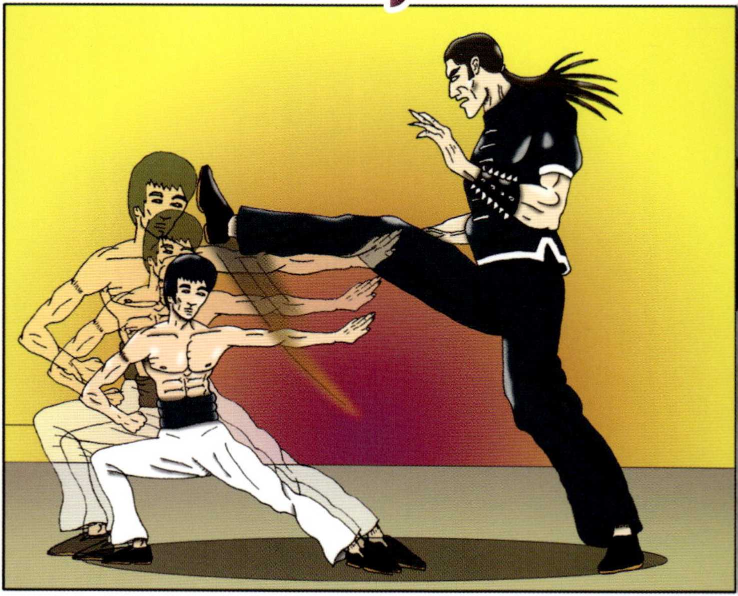

A mystical simplicity shines through his approach:

When the opponent expands, I contract.
When he contracts, I expand.

uiser

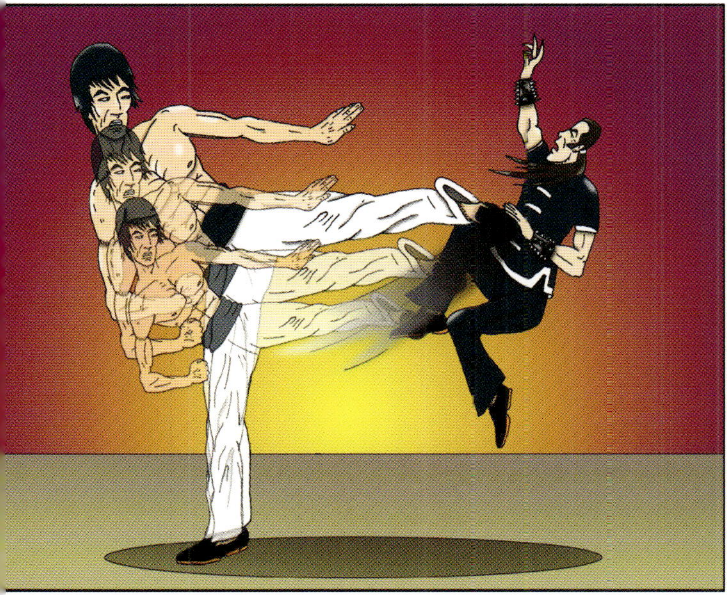

Sufferer

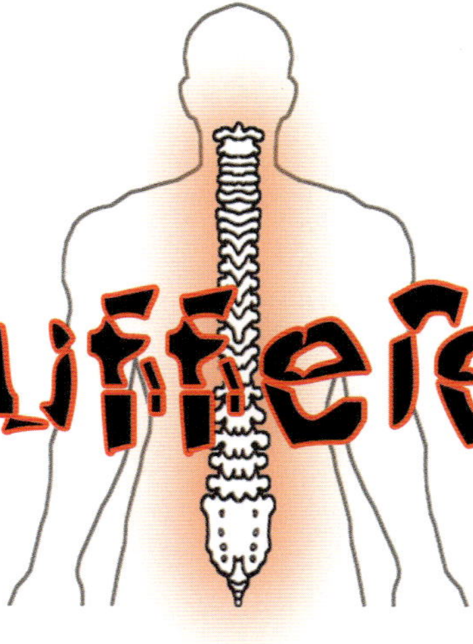

Lifting weights without a full warm-up,
Bruce injured his back.
Doctors diagnosed
a permanently damaged sacral nerve,
warning him:
"You'll never kick again!"
The man once nicknamed **Never Sits Still**
had to submit to
bed rest for months.

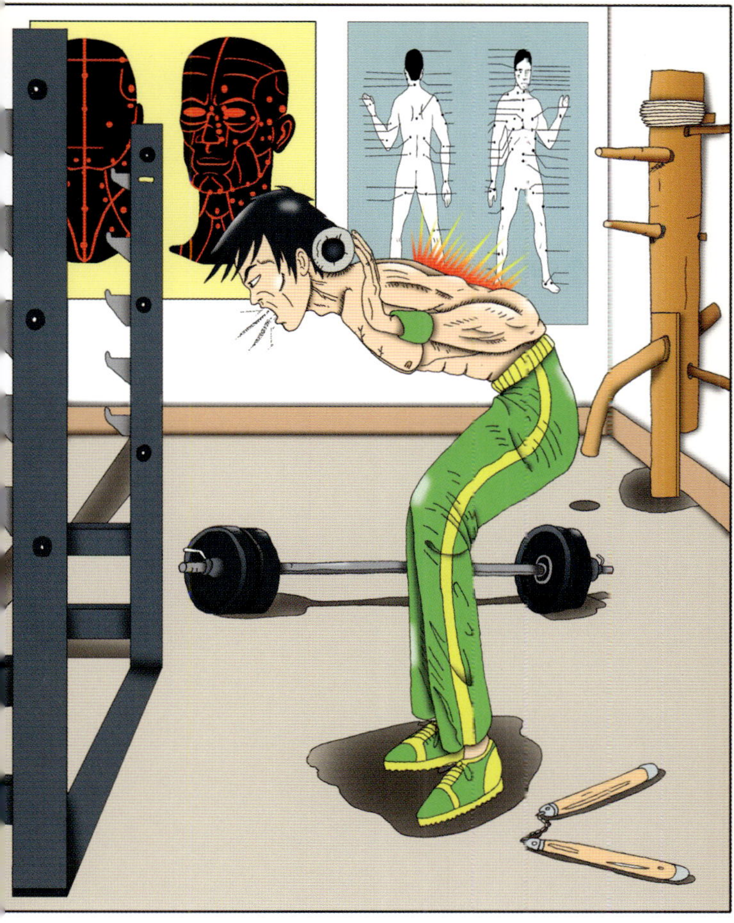

AUTHOR

While recuperating, Bruce wrote down his training and fighting anti-system. He gave it a Cantonese name that translates to the stop-hit way.

It took years to publish.

"It is indeed difficult to convey simplicity."

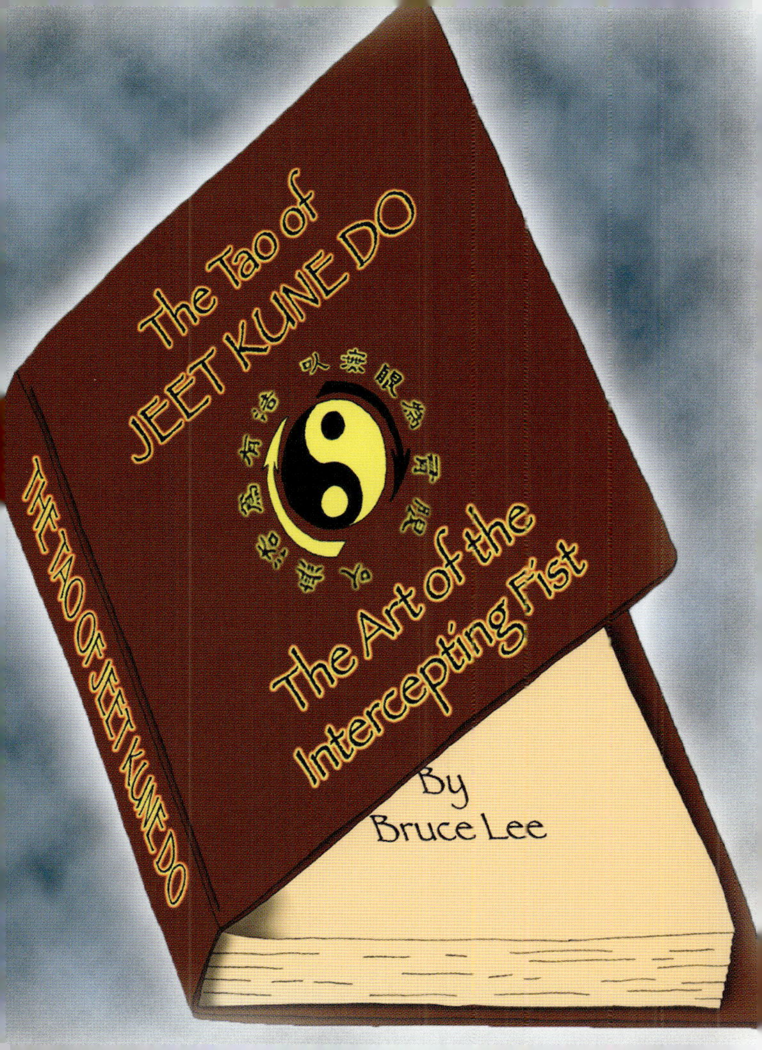

The Tao of
JEET KUNE DO
The Art of the
Intercepting Fist
By
Bruce Lee
THE TAO OF JEET KUNE DO

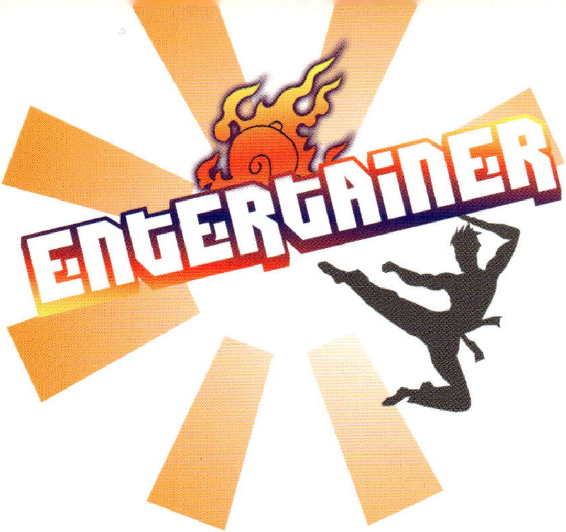

Ambitious to transmit his art on screen, Bruce bedazzled his fight repertoire with blood-freezing fight yells, wind-whipping nanchaku sticks, and spectacular aerial kicks.

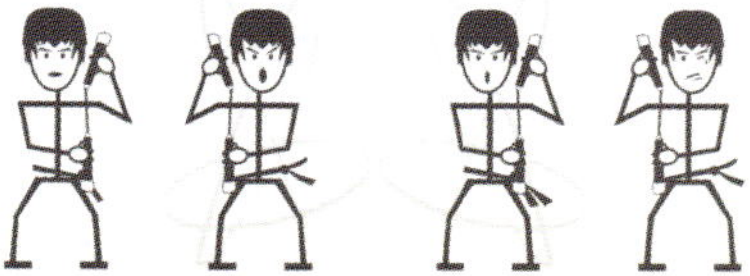

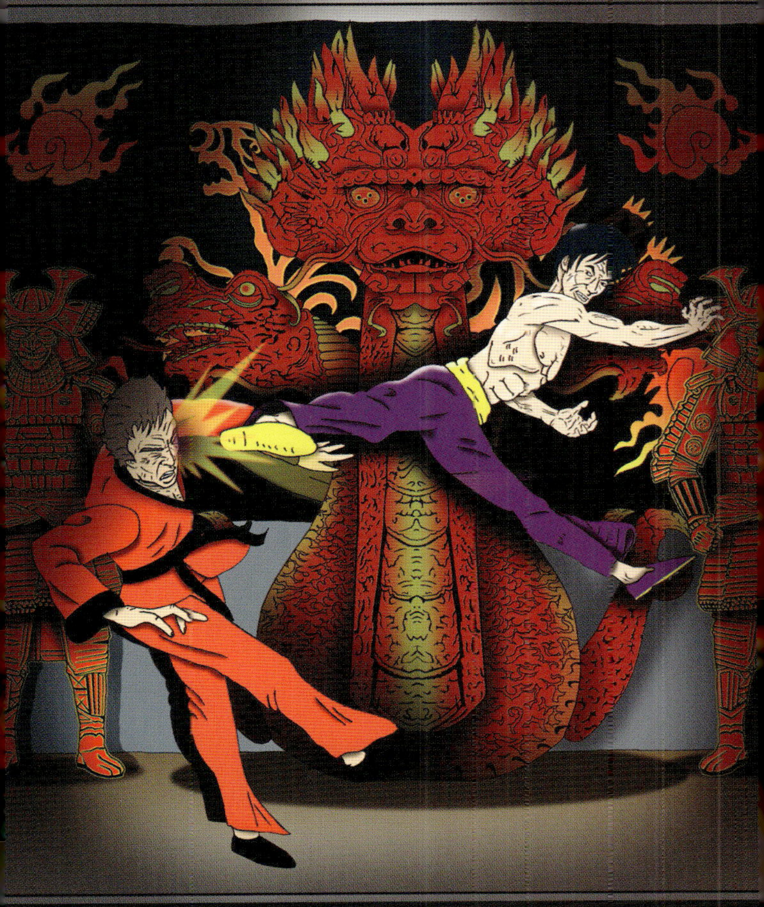

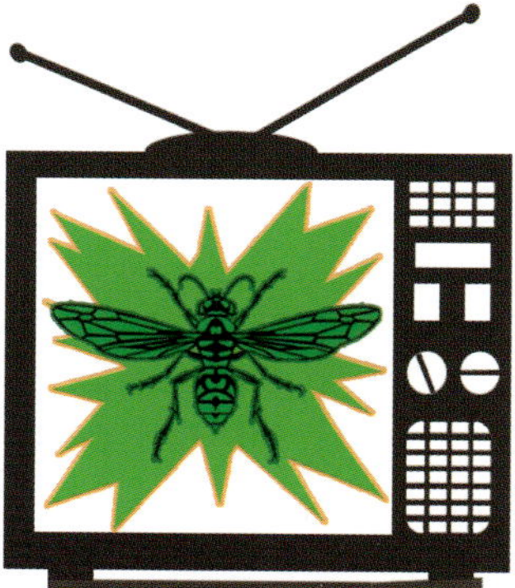

TV star

Mass audiences first witnessed Bruce Lee's fight mastery in

THE GREEN HORNET

His supporting role as Kato earned him modest fame and tv work in the U.S., but launched his star in Hong Kong.

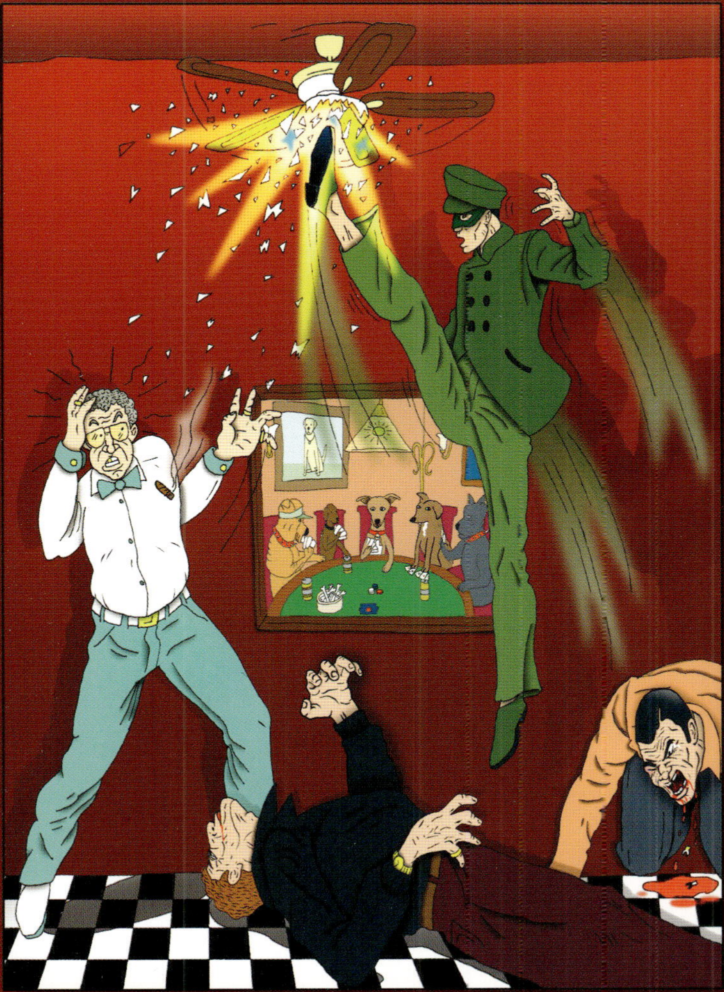

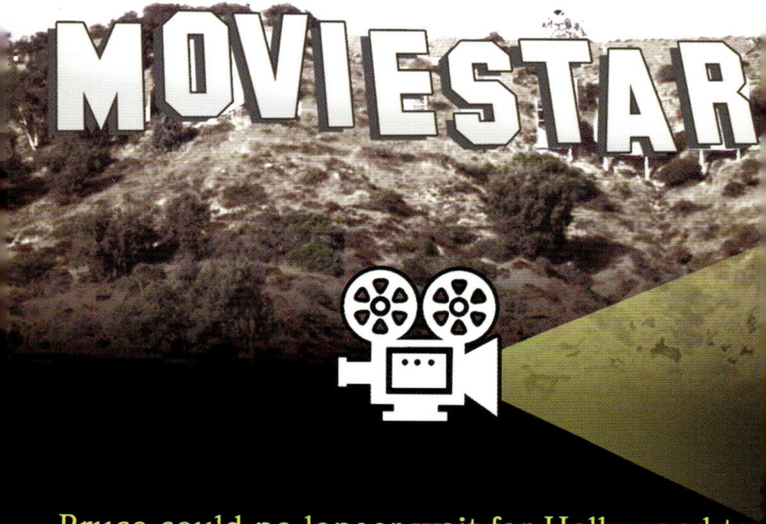

Bruce could no longer wait for Hollywood to offer him a breakout role, so he moved to Hong Kong and filmed four box office smashes in two years. In an unfinished fifth film, he tested his physical limits in a death match against his real-life student, 7-foot 2-inch tall Kareem Abdul Jabbar

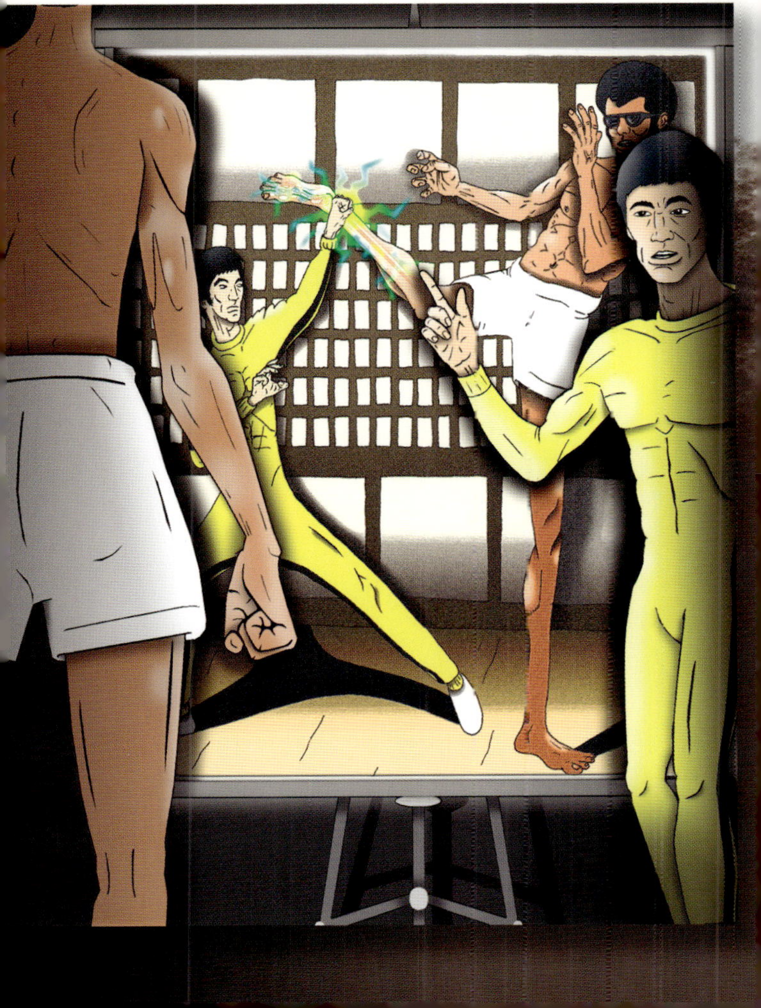

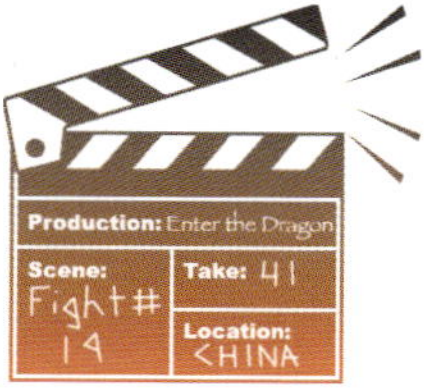

choreographer

Bruce revolutionized the martial art film genre. Instead of hiring actors to fake fight, he hired skilled fighters to brawl with unprecedented realism.

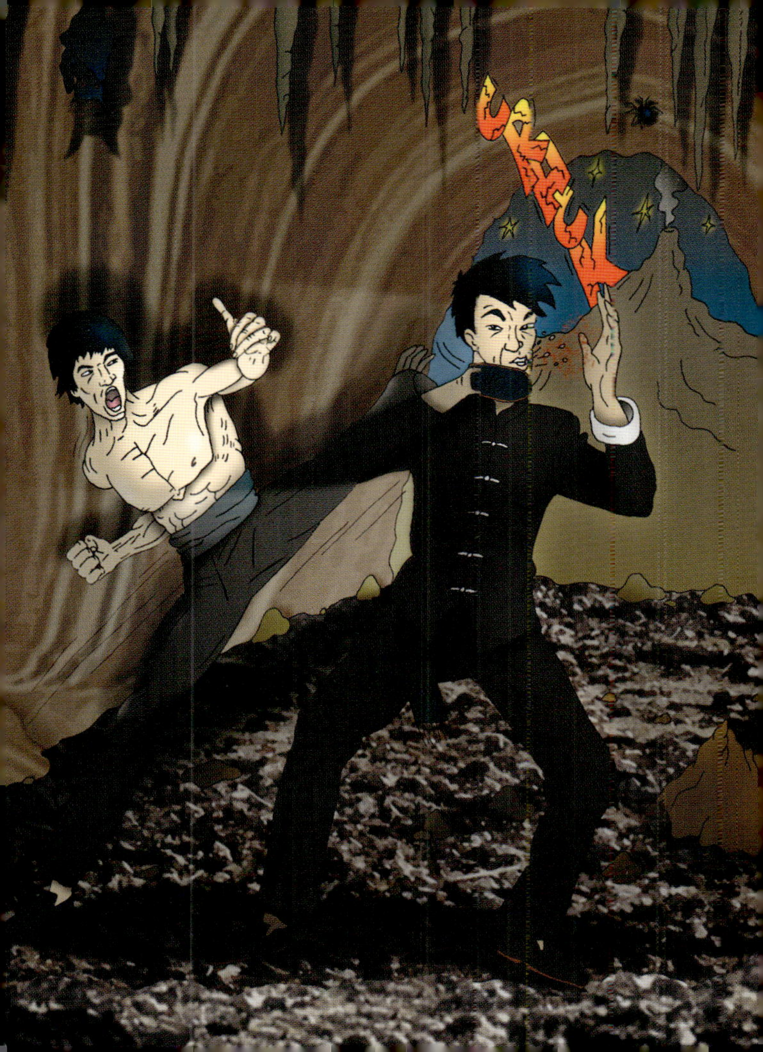

SPEEDSTER

His lightning fast moves made the air pop. He could swipe a coin out of your open palm and replace it with another before you could snap your fingers shut. On the set, he tapped a cobra's head and withdrew several times without getting bitten. Then he tapped once too often. De-venomized but not de-fanged, the snake bit Bruce's hand!

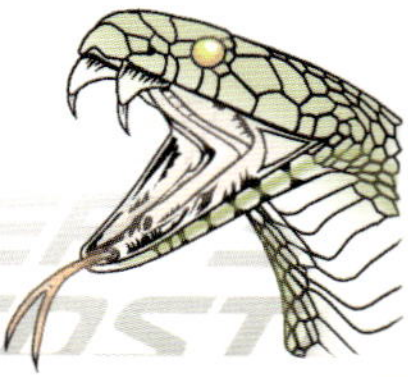

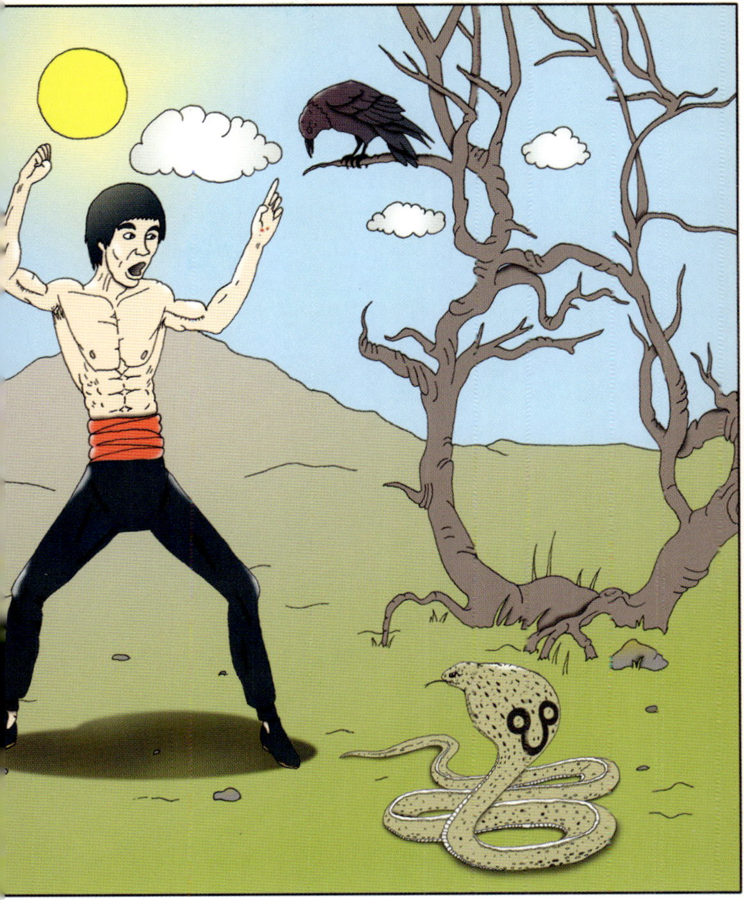

REAL DEAL

Martial artists pay
Bruce Lee utmost respect.
Chuck Norris is the toughest dude
in Texas. He was also Bruce's
student, spar, and co-star.

If you and Bruce Lee were really
going to fight to the death, who would win?

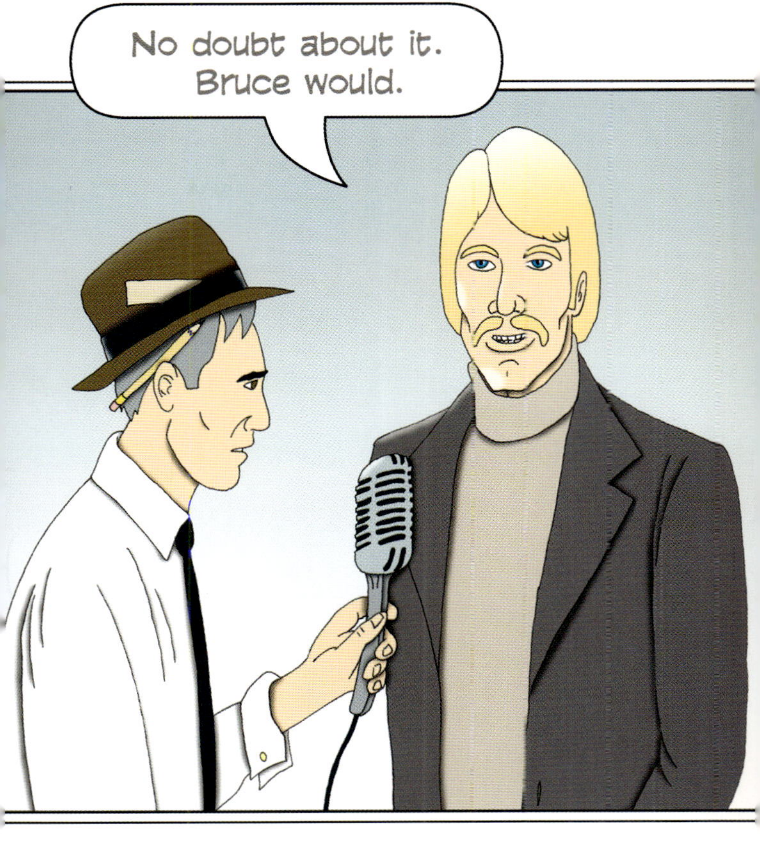
No doubt about it.
Bruce would.

ALPHA MALE

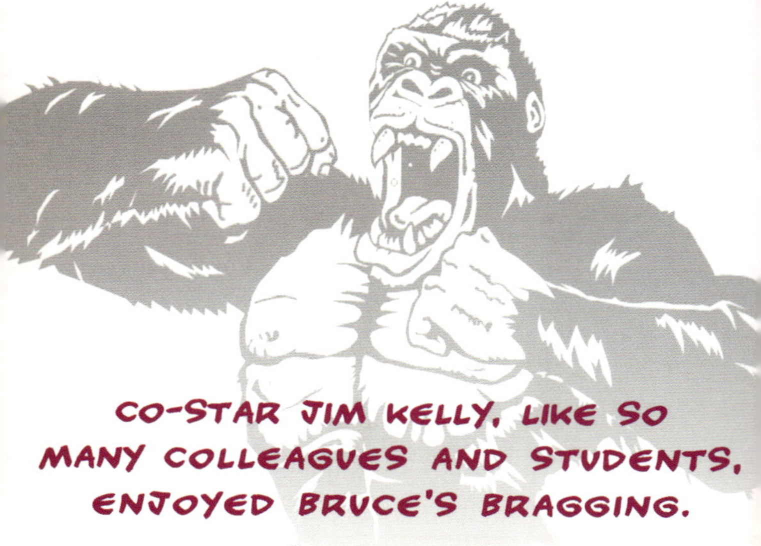

CO-STAR JIM KELLY, LIKE SO MANY COLLEAGUES AND STUDENTS, ENJOYED BRUCE'S BRAGGING.

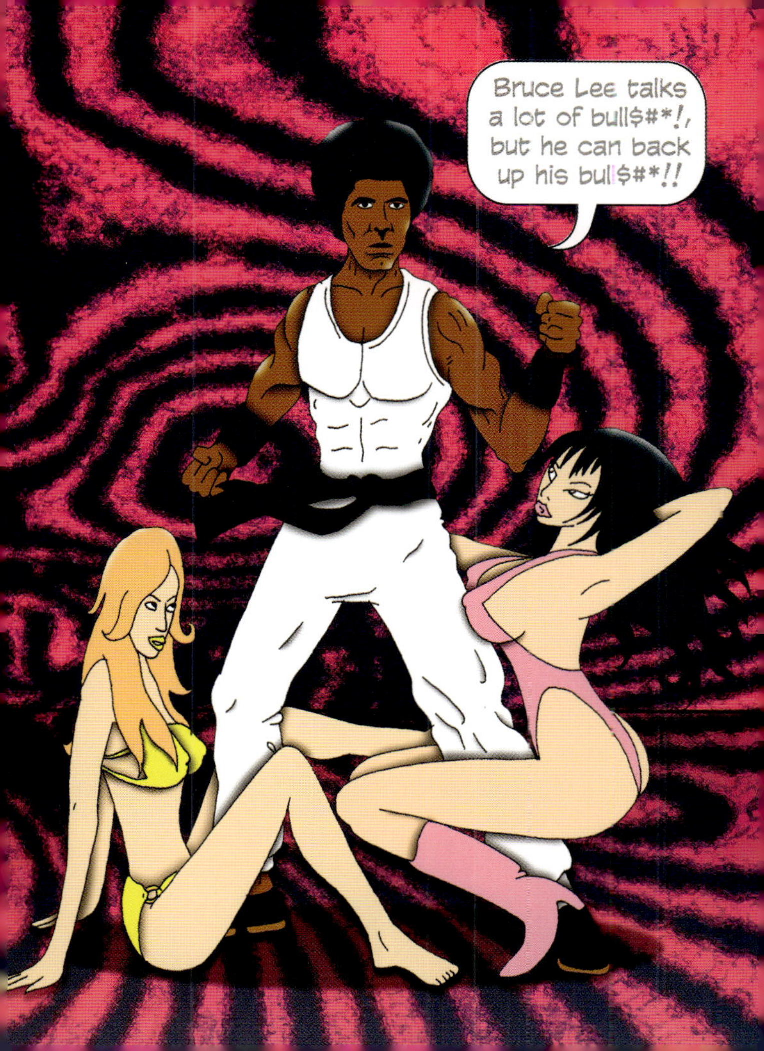
Bruce Lee talks a lot of bull$#*!, but he can back up his bull$#*!!

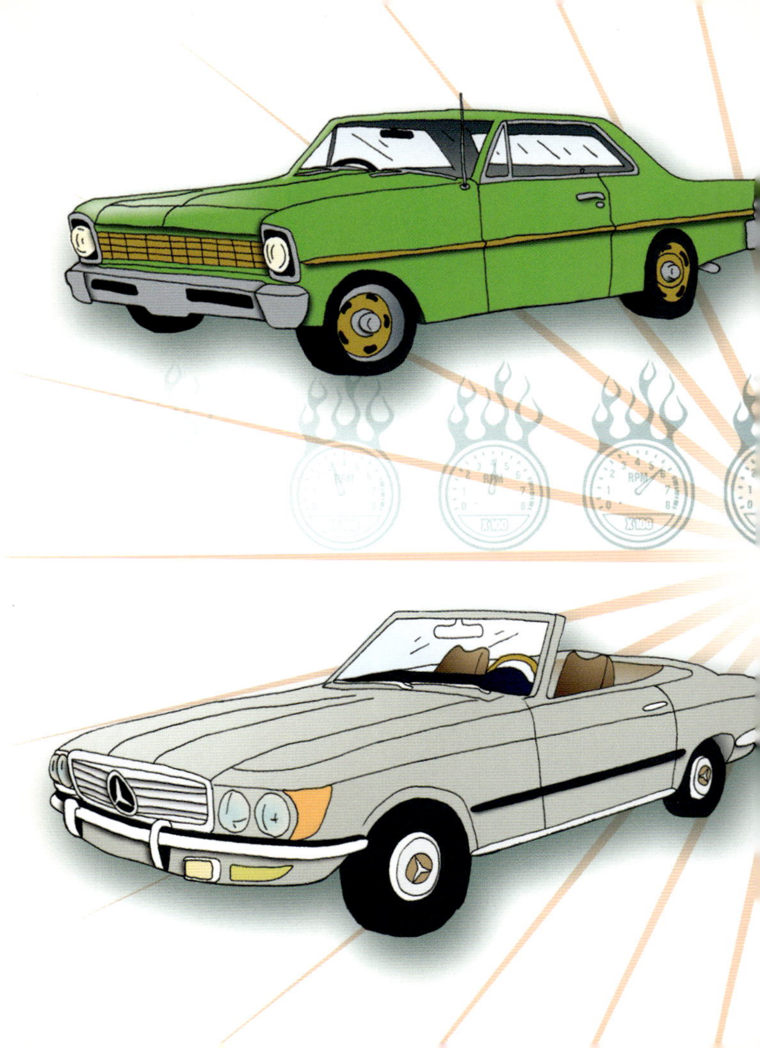
RPM
X100

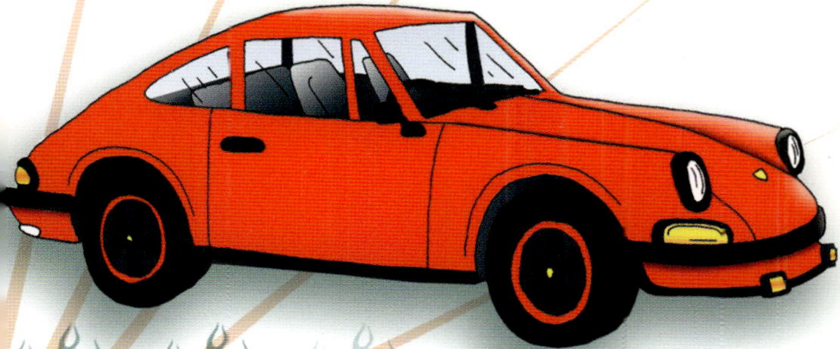

Cruiser

Bruce sported powerful cars

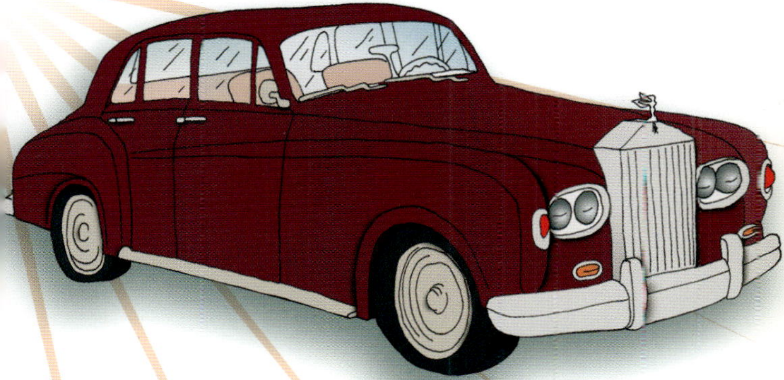

yogi

Bruce's daily commitment to meditation centered him within the swirl of ambition and fame.

"It helps occasionally to stop all thoughts."

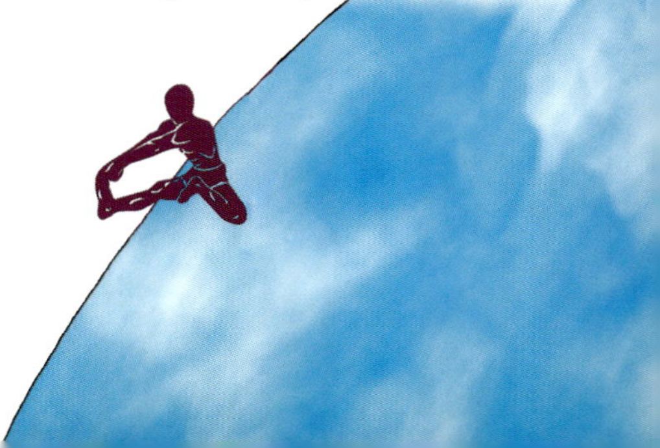

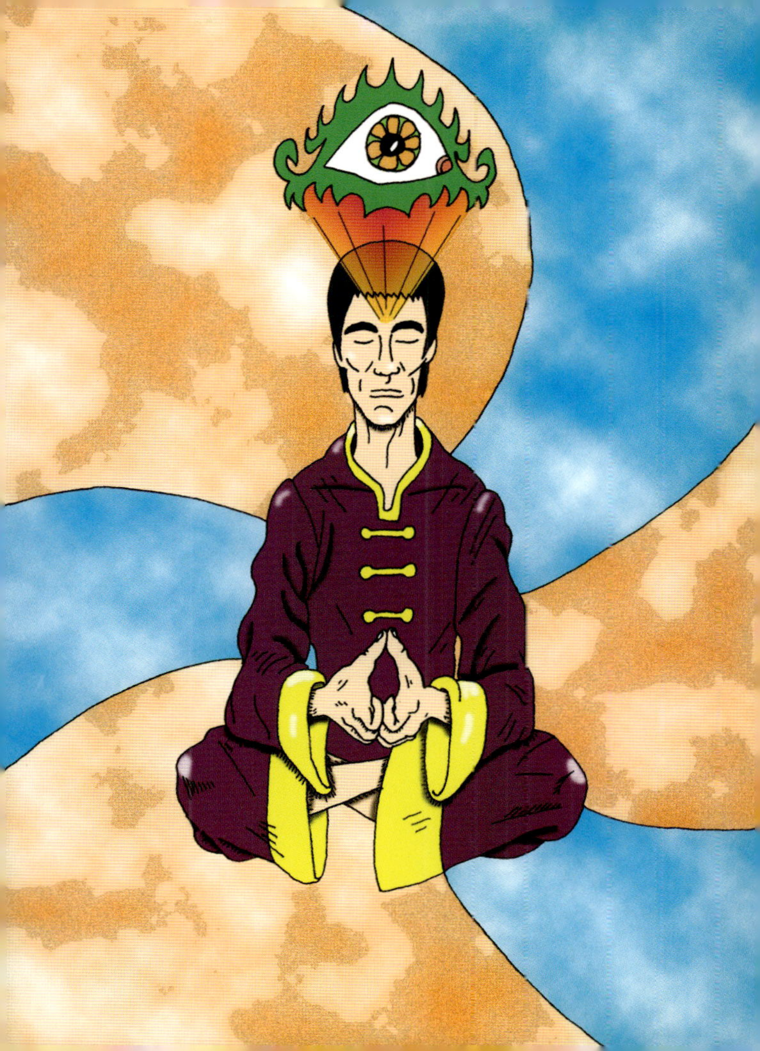

STONER

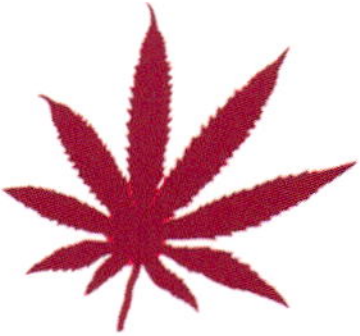

A Playboy article about hash cookies sparked Bruce's interest in a new way to mellow. *He chewed leaf and root, confiding to his doctor that it made*

"time slow down for a little while."

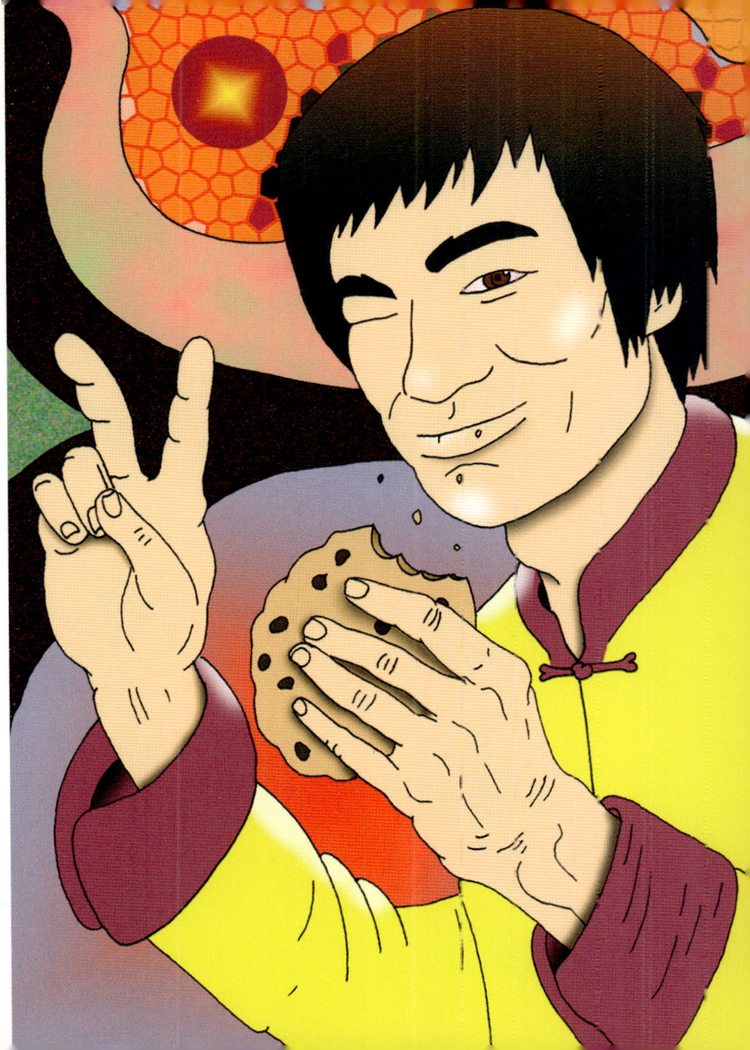

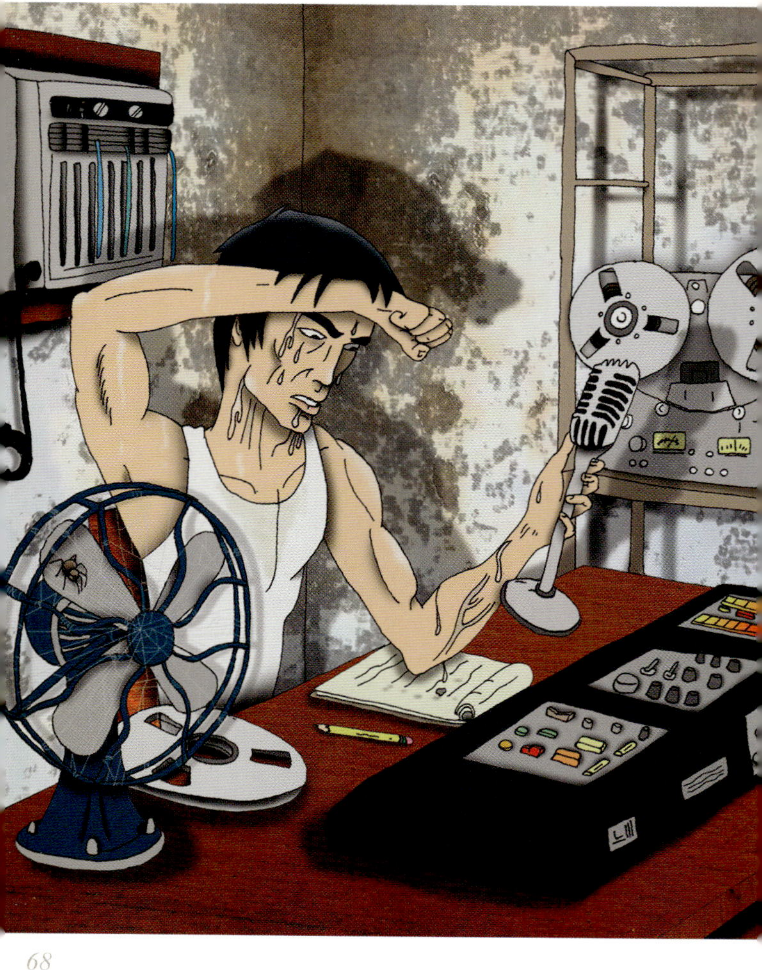

E N D U R E R

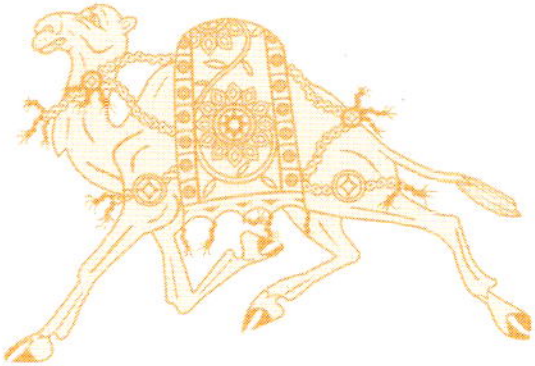

Actor, Producer, Writer, Choreographer,
Fighter, Teacher, Editor...

Bruce tried to do it all and make the

"f#@%ingest action motion picture that has ever been made."

He suffered dangerous injuries, weight-loss, sleeplessness, fight challenges, and at least one mysterious seizure. To cut the clearest soundtrack, Bruce chose to broil inside the sound editing room rather than activate the noisy fan.

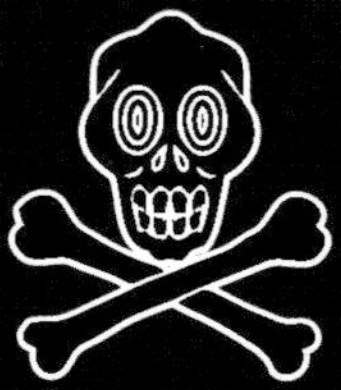

MORTAL

Days before the big premiere
of *Enter The Dragon,*
Bruce Lee lost
consciousness
and died at age 32.

Confused doctors
initially diagnosed
"death by
misadventure."

The official cause:
cerebral edema
(brain swelling)
likely caused by
an allergic reaction
to meprobamate
(pain killer)
and aspirin.

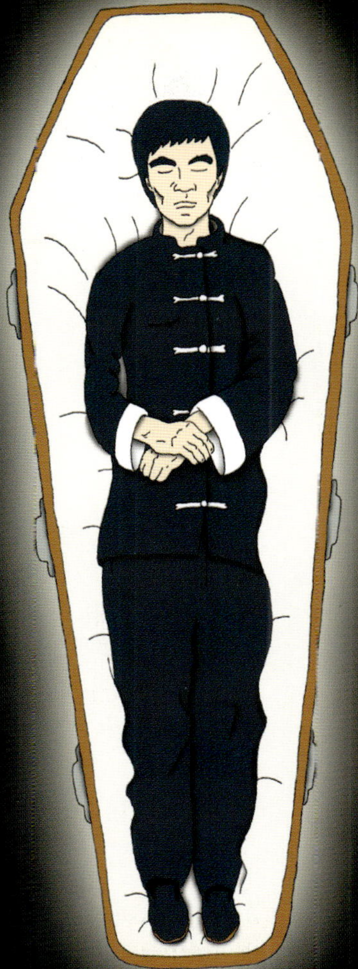

HERO

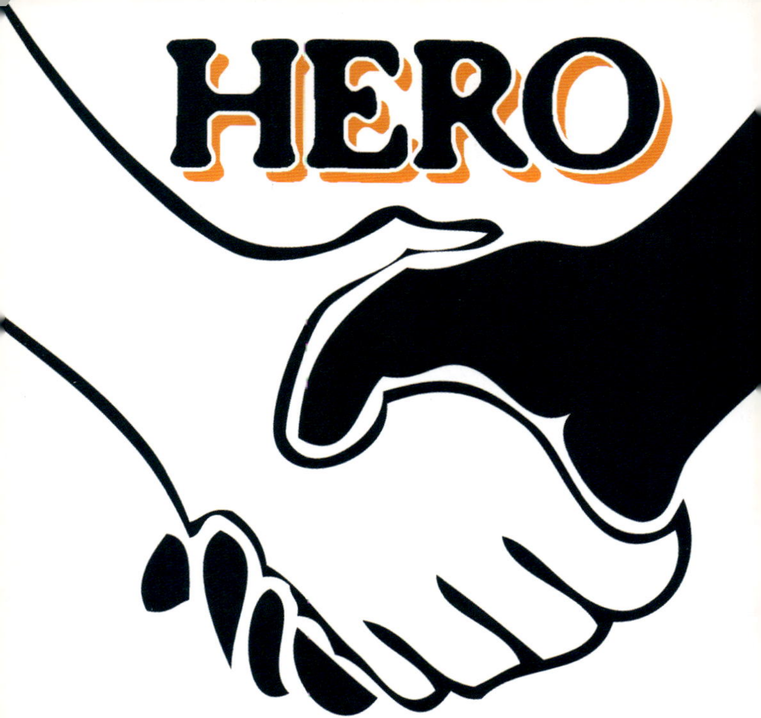

After the Serbian War, the former enemies agreed to erect a statue of the legendary fighter **poised to pummel.**

Why promote peace with a monument to a warrior? Because Bruce matched his sublime skills with sublime virtue: he fought only when morally necessary.

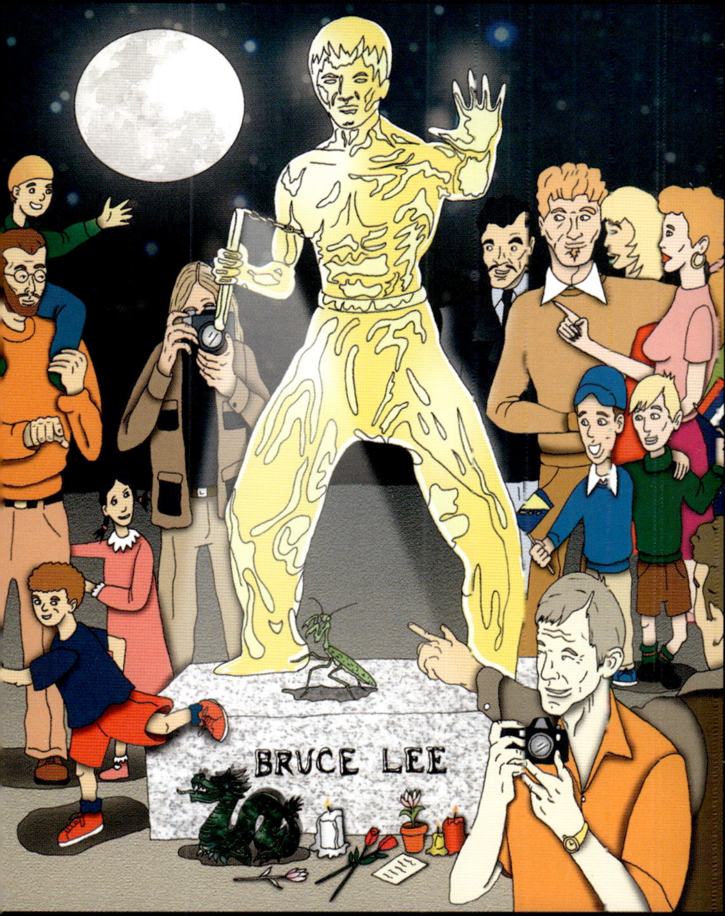
BRUCE LEE

His star shines on

Hollywood's Walk of Fame.

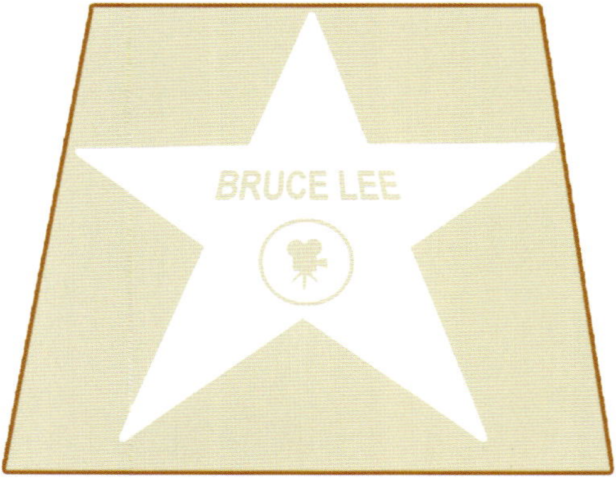

A larger than life bronze statue

in Hong Kong honors its hometown hero

with an accompanying plaque declaring:

BRUCE LEE
STAR OF THE CENTURY

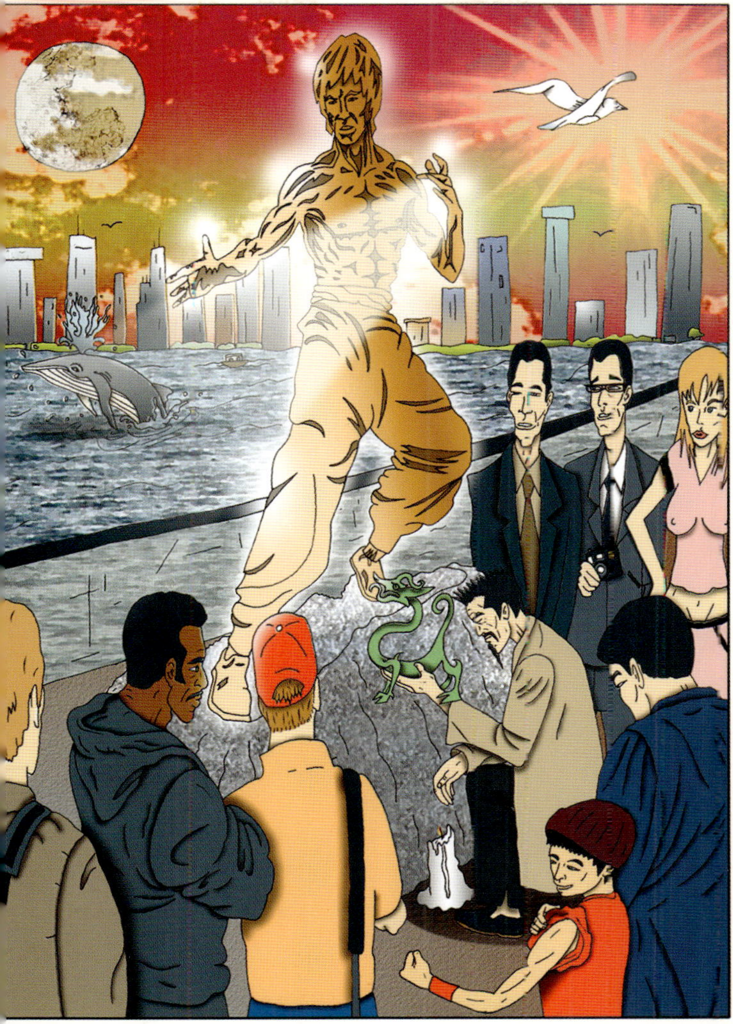

ANATOMY

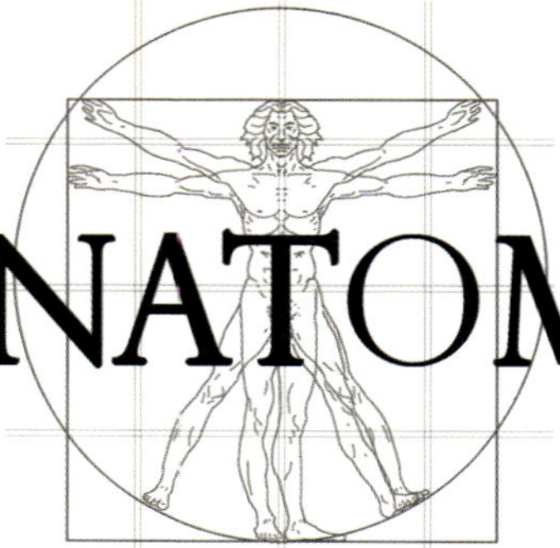

OF BRUCE THREE LEGS

Forearms raw and bruised
from hours intensely swinging
nanchaku sticks.

Bruce isometrically pressed against tables
and walls to summon energy,
or chi, into his biceps-triceps.

Rejected from Vietnam War draft
because of an undescended testicle.
Circumcised at age 22. Sired a son and daughter.

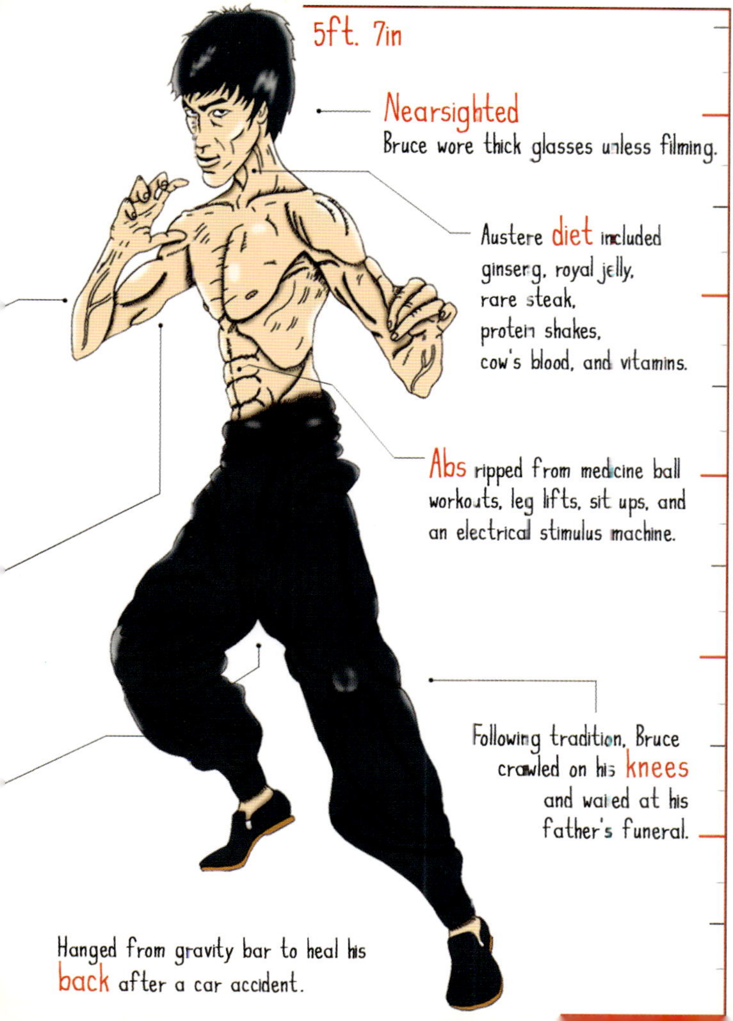
5ft. 7in
Nearsighted
Bruce wore thick glasses unless filming.
Austere diet included ginseng, royal jelly, rare steak, protein shakes, cow's blood, and vitamins.
Abs ripped from medicine ball workouts, leg lifts, sit ups, and an electrical stimulus machine.
Following tradition, Bruce crawled on his knees and waited at his father's funeral.
Hanged from gravity bar to heal his back after a car accident.

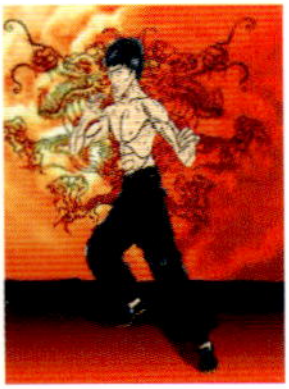

Bibliography

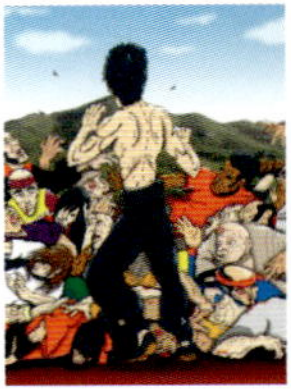

A. *Bruce Lee*, Linda Tagliaferro (Lerner Publications, Minneapolis 2000).

B. *Bruce Lee: A Warrior's Journey*, John R. Little (Contemporary, New York 2001).

C. *Bruce Lee: Artist of Life*, John Little, editor (Tuttle, Boston 1999).

D. *Bruce Lee: Fighting Spirit*, Bruce Thomas (Frog, Berkeley 1994).

E. *Bruce Lee: Letters of The Dragon*, John Little, editor (Tuttle, Boston 1998).

F. *Bruce Lee: The Celebrated Life of the Golden Dragon*, John Little, editor (Tuttle, Boston 2000).

G. *Bruce Lee: The Tao of the Dragon Warrior*, Louis Chunovic (St. Martin's Griffin, New York 1996).

H. *Bruce Lee's Fighting Method: Skill in Techniques*, B. Lee and M. Uyehara (Ohara, Burbank 1977).

I. *Bruce Lee's Fighting Method: Advanced Techniques*, B. Lee and M. Uyehara (Ohara, Santa Clarita 1977).

J. *Bruce Lee's Fighting Method: Self-Defense Techniques*, B. Lee and M. Uyehara (Ohara, Burbank 1976).

K. *The Legend of Bruce Lee*, Alex Ben Block (Dell, New York 1974).

L. *The Legendary Bruce Lee*, Editors of Black Belt Magazine (Ohara, Santa Clarita 1986).

M. *The Pocket Essential Bruce Lee*, Simon B. Kenny (Pocket Essentials, UK 2001).

N. *The Warrior Within*, John Little (Contemporary Books, Chicago 1996).

O. *The Wisdom of Bruce Lee*, Felix Dennis and Roger Hutchinson (Pinnacle Books, New York 1976).

P. *They Died Too Young: Bruce Lee*, Jon E. Lewis (Chelsea, Philadelphia 1998).

Q. *Bruce Lee a symbol of unity in divided Bosnia town*, by Reuters on September 12, 2005 at htttp://reuters.co.uk.

R. *Bosnia unveils Bruce Lee bronze*, by BBC News on November 26, 2005 at http://bbc.co.uk.

S. *Mostar's Little Dragon: How Bruce Lee became a symbol of peace in the Balkans*, by Alexander Zaitchik in the April 2006 issue of Reason.com at http://reason.com/archives/2006/04/01/mostars-little-dragon.

T. *The Hard, Short Rise of Bruce Lee*, by Vincent Mao on June 3, 2008 in Investor's Business Daily.

Source Notes

Punk *"As a kid in Hong Kong..."* [K:21, L:10; P:7]; *"I was extremely mischievous, aggressive, hot-tempered and fierce"* [C:34; D:91; 269 (*"punk"*); F:9 (*"From boyhood to adolescence, I was a bit of a troublemaker.... I was extremely mischievous and aggressive"*); G:1 (pugnacious)]; weapons [D:25 (carried concealed blade/ steel chain but rarely used); L:10-12 (school kids improvised weapons)]. Similarly, see A:22-24 (schoolboy fights), 28 (knocked out boy's tooth).

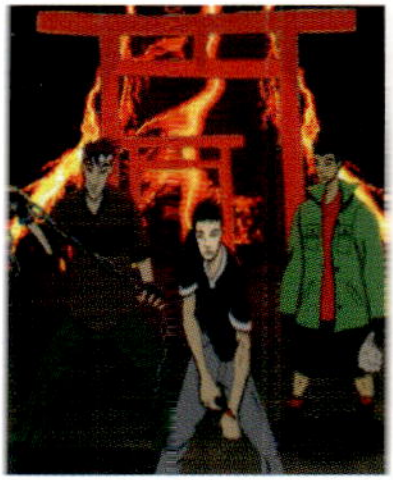

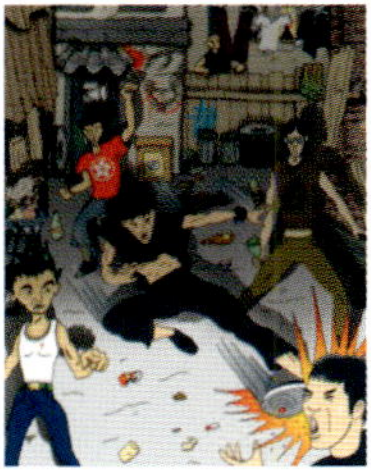

Seeker started kung fu when he *"began to feel insecure"* [L:10], despised losing [A:12; D:xvi (unable to place second), 25 (unbearable, furious loser), 27 (fight diary), 271 (win by any means); K:47 ("intolerant" of intentions "for anything less than all out victory"), 51 ("anything to win"), 88 (winning his "single interest" and "greatest joy"); L:12; P:9 (couldn't stand when a spar hit him with good shot)], bullies [D:14; P:8], sought self-defense skills [A:24; K:19; L:10-11; M:15], *"I wondered..."* [F:9; K:21; L:10; O:19-20], *wing chun* kung fu lessons [A:24, E:33 note 6; D:14; G:1, 39; M:15].

Student *sticking hands* [D:18, 121, 281 (sticking hands breeds spontaneous flow), 282 (develops contact reflex); G:1], blindfold [D:18, 121 (improves kinesthetic awareness); L:12], "Follow nature and don't interfere with her ways. Let your mind do the counter movement without deliberation" [C:16; N:46-47; O:23], "Learn the art of detachment. Just relax" [C:16; G:1; N:46; O:23].

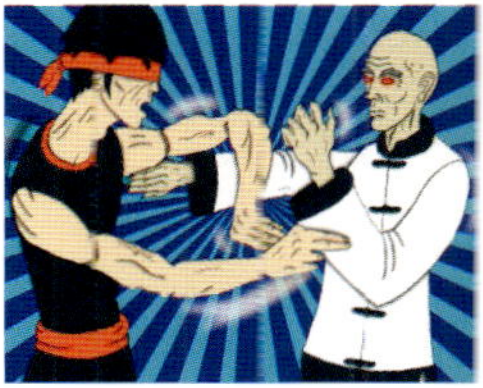

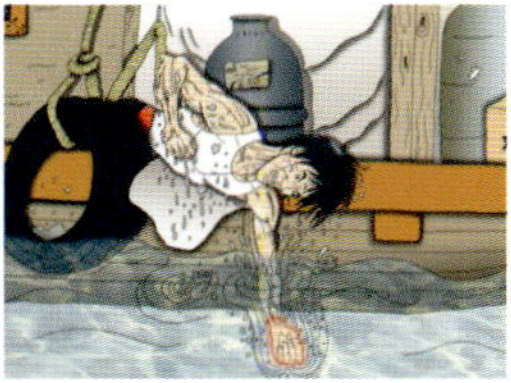

Struggler D:234 (*"There are no limits. Only plateaux"*), progress stalled [C:16], took a break [D:25; N:46], took a boat ride [C:16], lashed at the sea [C:17; D:26; N:47].

Visionary *"I struck it just now..."* [A:26-27; C:17, 50; D:288; E:37-38; G:2; M:32-33; N:47; O:23].

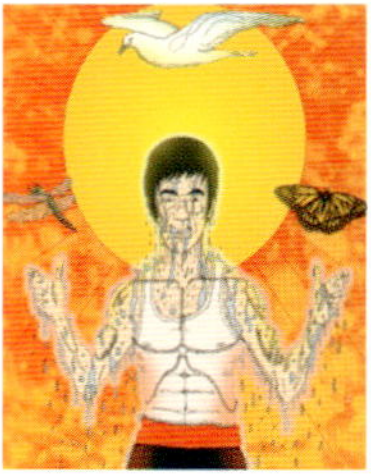

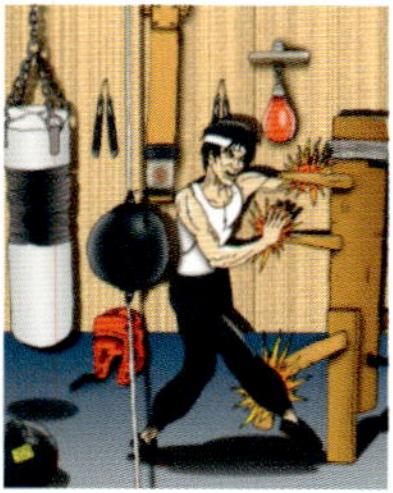

Perfectionist repeat to perfection [B:116; D:157 (practiced one kick 300 times); E:99; K:38 (perfectionist), 87 (ego driven); L:65, 92; O:51, 114; P:14 (physical perfection)], trained fanatically [D:231 (indefatigable drive); G:x, 38; J:7, 11; K:39 (multi-tasker: exercised, flexed, stretched, and read simultaneously); L:39, 150; M:29;O:56-57; P:18 (learned through teaching others)], self-knowledge [B:57, 72, 163, 237-238; C:151 (really fighting own ego, fear, blockages), 223-244 in general; D:101 (self-study), 263 ("actively work on self-knowledge"); F:144 (Bruce: "*Ultimately, martial art is the expression of oneself*"); L:67, 116; N:xix, 90 (ultimate human goal); O:30 (liberation through physical achievement)], "*How can I...*" [A:27; B:57, 112; N:95; O:64], stuffed garage/home with equipment [G:23-24; K:49-50; L:16, 119, 158; O:51, 61].

Defender self-defense as purpose of all training [J:6], *"Always keep yourself well-covered..."* [L:56; O:59], protective gear [B:36; D:277; E:66, 111 (head, hands, chest, shins and knees), 123; F:68K:49-50, 94; L:19, 50-51; O:61], full-contact workouts [B:38-39; D:65 (real sparring most valuable); E:41; G:25 photo, 38; J:7; L:59, 64].

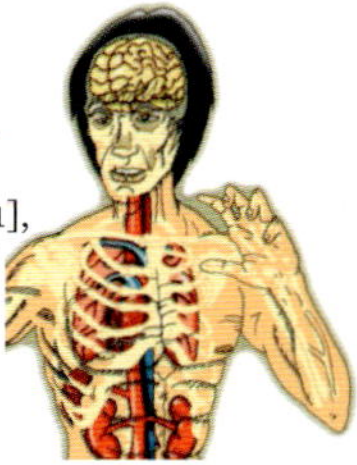

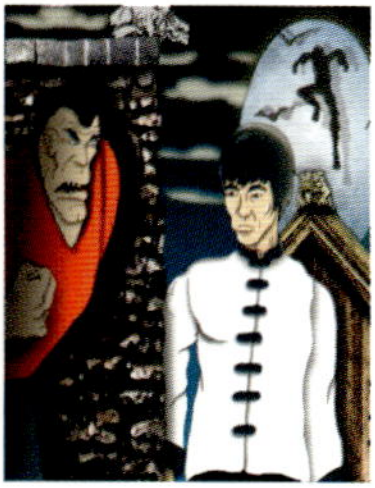

Anticipator vigilance [C:22 (prevent surprise attacks, hear footsteps, watch shadows), 179 ("altogether alert awareness"); D:283 (intention + awareness = mastery); F:78 ("*...bring the mind into sharp focus....*") and 121 ("*To be on the alert means to be deadly serious*"); G:xi (infallible awareness of position); J:11; O:78-79 (surprise assailants)], *"A good martial artist does not become tense..."* [B:59, 159; F:118; M:33; N:162].

Kicker generally [I:67-91], *"When you can kick so..."* [D:64; K:49; O:58], the forward leg [C:23 ("given a choice, I would always use the leg"); K:46], longest weapon [B:39; E:99; J:9-10 photos; K:46], wins against knee or groin [M:29], transfers massive energy [B:39 (damaging); C:23; O:58], *"compared to your left jab"* [B:39].

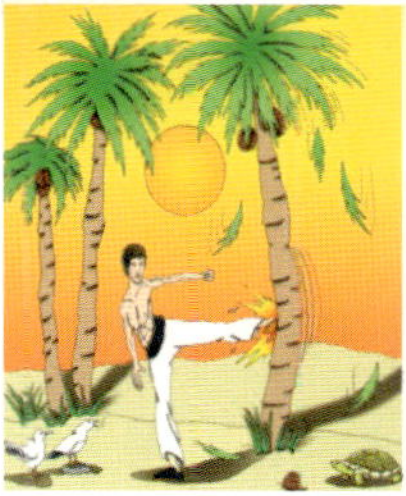

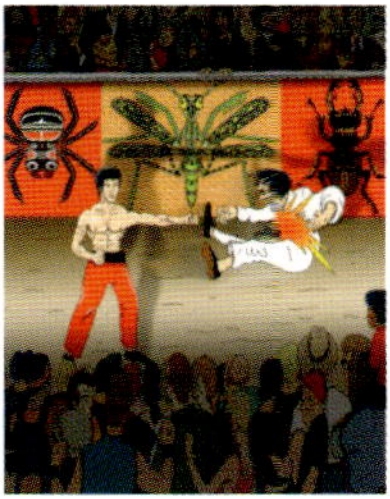

Puncher abbreviated from *"power of the kick and punch..."* [E:75, 77 (turn hip and shoulder into impact); H:19, 30 (elements of punch skill); L:56; O:58], one-inch punch [A:7; B:43; D:56-57; G:22 (demonstrating applied focus), 28-29; K:95; L:20-21; M:19, 54-55], screen test [A:8, 37; D:67-73; G:32; K:36; L:71-72; M:19, 90; O:121-122].

Jogger chasing inferior opponent [B:30-31; D:62-63; E:82 note 23; L:6 M:19-20, 30, 91; O:86-87; P:14], fittest man in world [D:204], intensive, daily exercise [D:63; L:47, 146 (speed, agility, power, flexibility, accuracy)], jogging [B:152; D:63; E:111; L:18, 72; O:52-59], "*king of all exercises*" [L:53], serious fighter intent upon hard sparring [L:53; O:54-55], dog named Bo [E:82 note 16, 93] sometimes confused with friend's similarly-named dog, Bobo [D:63; L:34, 53; O:55].

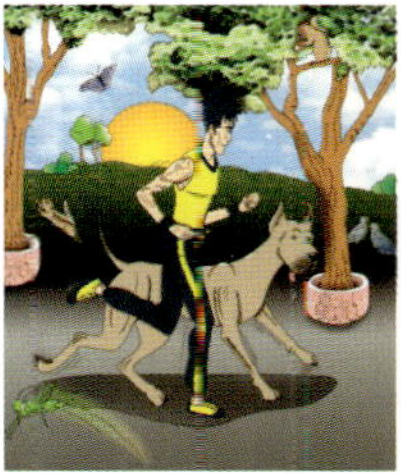

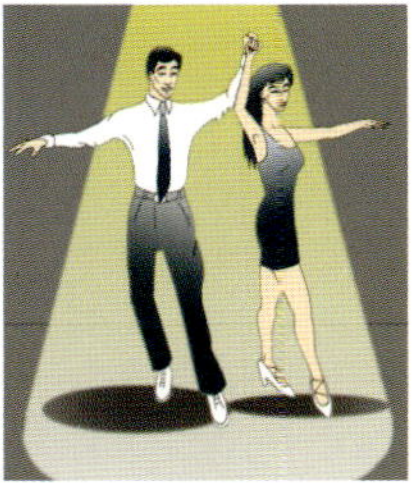

Dancer welcomed any discipline [G:20-38; O:52-59], footwork [H:12, 26 (precision)], tai chi, fencing, wrestling, savate, archery, skipping rope boxing, running with leg weights, judo insect mimicry, ballet, cha-cha [A:23; D:23, 96-97, 283 (dancing affords "continual flow of movement"); G:4, 38; L:9; M:15], perfecting 100 steps [D:23; G:4].

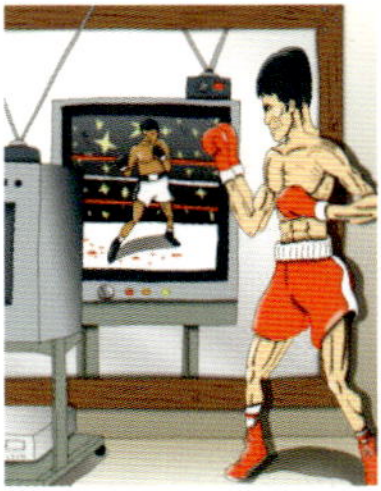

Rythmist broken/irregular rhythm [B:34; D:283 (studied Indian music for improvised melodies/rhythms); E:44 (fast, efficient interception of opponent's rhythm), 72 ("*classically fast and snappy*" movement incorrectly sets steady rhythm that helps opponent); G:xiii (requires: coolness; light/ smooth/fast feet; off-beat movement); H:22 (to confuse opponent about distance); L:44, 57], the gap [E:43, 57, 99; K:50; L:57; O:61], feint-strike-retreat [H:17, 19-20], Muhammad Ali [D:96-97; G:4; L:17-18, 127; P:28].

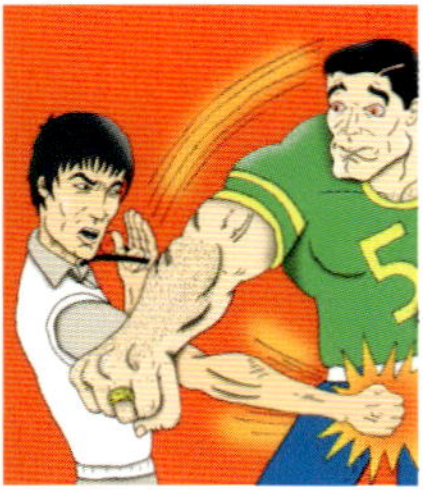

Exploder thick glasses for extreme nearsightedness [A:15; G:ix, 9], unsuspecting punk [D:51], unleash [K:85 (totality of physical and mental efforts yielded extraordinary life force), 96-97 (could release stupendous chi at will); O:58 (deliver with controlled anger)], hallmark of Bruce's onscreen characters [G:51; K:75; L:84], patience [B:154 (wait for attackers to come to you); D:xviii (personally, forever impatient); E:144 ("*The damn thing is I want to do something now!*"); K:47 (final five years he "trained, taught, read, dreamed and above all choked with frustration")].

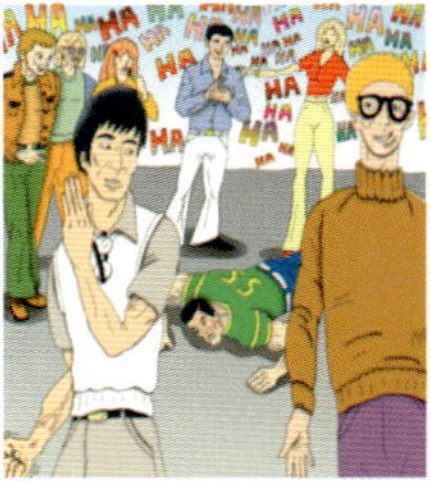

Psychologist see [C:21 (psychological advantage), 71-90 (generally), 198 ("technical skill is to be subordinate to the psychic training"); D:121 (feel opponent's intent, then neutralize); G:20 (emphasized attitude); H:19 (conceal intentions); K:46; N:158 ("viciously attack" biggest first to intimidate whole gang)], "*...beaten by a nerd...*" [D:51], mental and physical [M:32].

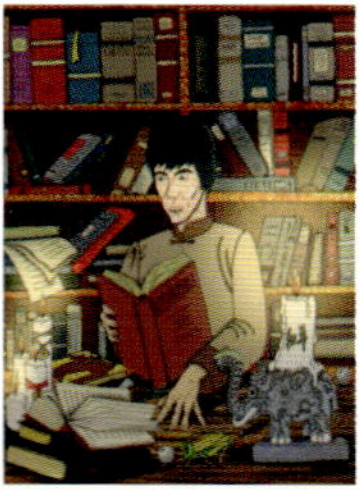

Philosopher read widely [A:15, 47; B:29; D:75, 93, 96; G:38 (eclectic); L:119; M:32-33; N:7, 19]; studied in college [B:23, 32, 46; F:65], synthesize best philosophy and techniques from all martial arts [C:38; E:81 note 10 (spiritual and technical root truths); G:20]; "using *no way as way*" [B:54; M:30], affinity with Krishnamurti [A:47; B:47-48; D:75, 96, 270-271; F:90 ("Truth is a pathless road"); G:39; M:32].

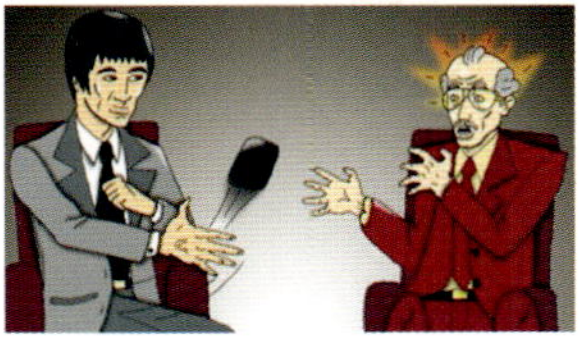

Iconoclast martial arts rebel [B:93; K:121 ; O:35-36 (*"I don't push. I punch."*)], *"classical mess"* [C:29, 184; F:90 (*"individual is always more important than the system"*); K:29; L:42; O:28 (*"baloney"*), 47 (*"formulas inhibit freedom"*)], *"blindly rehearsing systematic routines and stunts..."* [C:30; K:29; L:42; O:26 -29], *"... no way a person is going to fight you in the street with a set pattern"* [L:6], *"That is directness...."* [D:95 (threw object at student's head), 267 ("if in doubt, straight blast"); K:40 (threw nunchakus at brother's head) to make the point; L:46, 63; O:40, 61 (function first)].

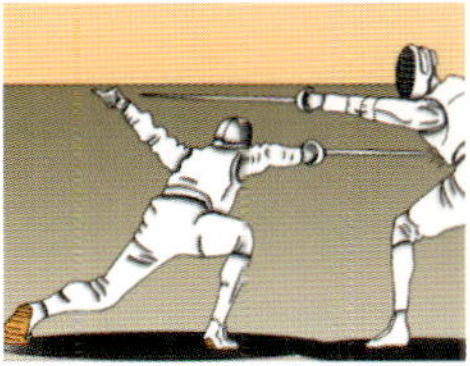

Economist economist [D:81], "Economy of Form" [E:98 (wastes no motion)], super-efficient street fighting [B:152; D:105; E:44, 110; F:68; G:20; K:13, 39, 41 (stripped to essentials); L:42; O:36-37], most with the least [B:26 (minimum motion for direct expression), 38 (ornamental motion discarded), 114 (looked to science to determine the most efficient way to deliver maximum impact force to an opponent); C:23 ("apply most effective weapon as soon as possible to the most vulnerable point of your enemy"); D:18 (maximum anguish, minimum movement), 181 (simple, direct, no facial expression = "controlled cruelty"), 264; E:40, 77 (simplicity = "minimum lines and energy" to express maximum); J:21; L:43, 46, 64 68, 146; M:30; N:xiv (urging simplicity), 119; O:22 (gentleness = neutralize opponent with minimal exertion)], stop-hit fencing technique [M:27-28], offense and defense [B:39 (intercepting attack with one's own attack), 97; D:121 (simultaneous block-hit); E:60 (combo of wing chun, fencing, and boxing); K:40 (no passive blocks reach opponent and strike); L:44].

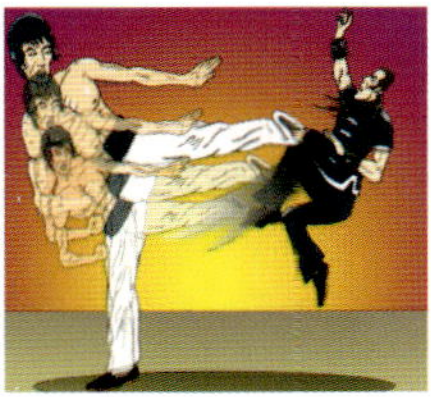

Improviser formlessness [B:95; D:86 (fighter becomes "complement to the opponent's energy"), 270 (adapt and play styles mid-fight), 281 (sticking hands breeds spontaneous flow); F:34 (*"When you get into a fight, everybody reacts differently."*), 101 (*"If the enemy is cool, stay cooler than him. If the enemy moves, move faster than him."*); K:50 (superlative "improvisational ability"); M:31 (*"smooth, rhythmic expression of smashing the guy before he hits you with any method available"*); N:44 (instantaneous adaptation); O:12], *"When the opponent expands"* [A:25-26; D:188; F:125; M:33, 45].

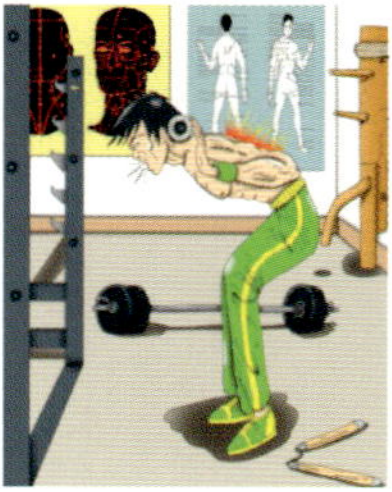

Sufferer lifting weights [A:44; G:39; L:22], damaged sacral nerve [A:45; B:44; E:172 note 6; G:39; P:18; M:92], "You'll never do kung fu again!" [G:39], nicknamed *Never Sits Still* [A:15; D:8; K:17; M:15], months of bed rest [A:45-47; B:44; L:10; P:18].

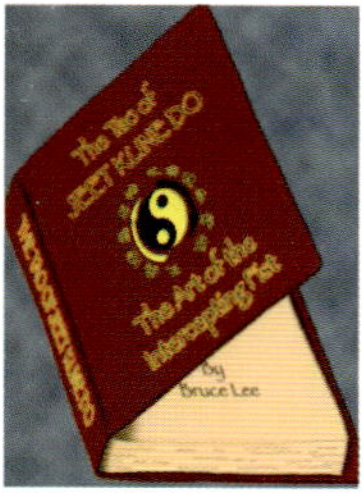

Author recuperation writing [G:39], anti-system [G:xvi, 39], jeet kun do or stop-hit way [D:81; G:20; K:39 ("jeet"=stalk/intercept; "kune"=fist/style; "do"=ultimate way/reality); M:27-28; N:xiii (aka "intercepting fist that follows the way of nature")], published posthumously [L:51; P:19], *"...difficult to convey simplicity"* [L:51; N:130; O:45], Bruce added arrows to traditional yin-yang symbol [G:28; C:46 ("ceaseless interplay"); G:33, 37 (on business cards); C:45 (photo of Bruce posing beneath symbol); D:19 (casket covered with symbolic flower arrangement); G:33].

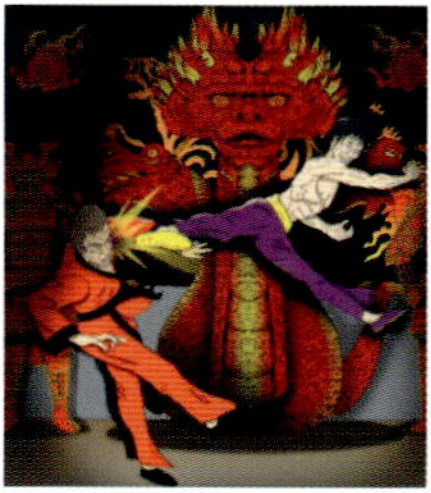

Entertainer commercial audience [E:44; K:44; O:95], fighting yell [K:80 ("Kiai!" scares others, tenses self, and summons chi)], aerial kicks [B:10; D:76 (flashy, flying kicks); L:32-33; M:29], nanchakus [O:42-43]; versus real fight [L:69; M:8, 29 (wouldn't rule high kick out if optimal)].

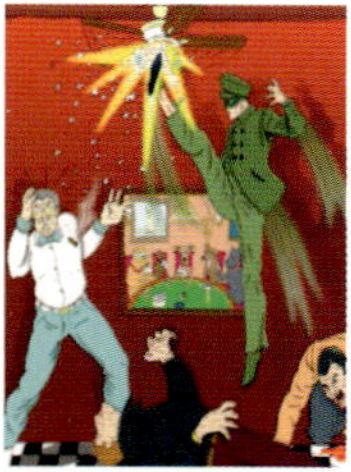

TV Star *The Green Hornet* [A:38-41; G:31, 33], one season only [A:41; B:32; D:78; F:24; K:43; L:34; M:27; P:17], *Kcto* [L:40], small tv parts [B:61; D;102-103; G:42-43; P:34], Hong Kong stardom [A:51; G:41, 54; K:69-70; M:37, 93 (national hero); P:19-20], returned to Hong Kong [A:48-49; G:43, 61; K:69, 73; O:130-131].

Movie Star smashed Asian box office records [B:3-4, 66, 69; D:131, 139, 169; G:54, 61, 81; K:89, 92; L:28, 74, 84; M:46, 48-49], Kareem Abdul Jabbar [A:62-63 (7'2" student "gigantic challenge" for 5'7" Bruce); B:69, 82-83; G:95, 100-101; L:21], yellow suit [B:93 (comfy, nontraditional outfit signaled independence from traditional martial art schools)].

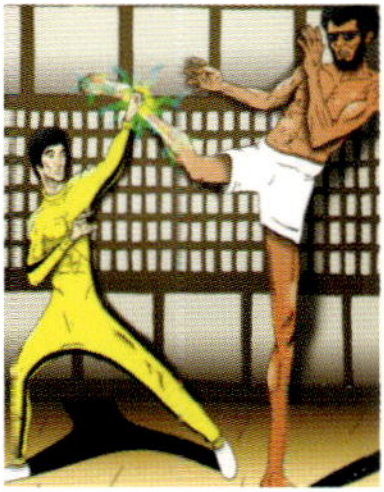

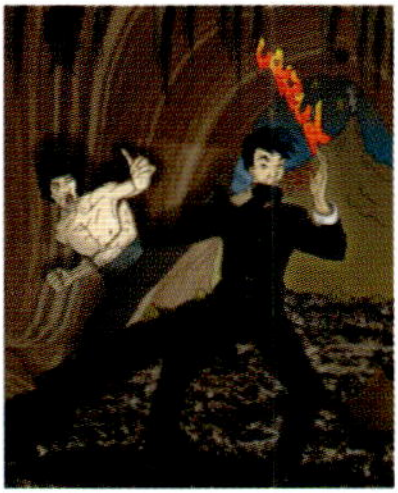

Choreographer pioneer [A:55; D:246; K:73-74; L:23, 84, 87, 93; M:11, 39], hired martial actors [B:77, 79; D:158; G:59; N112-113], young Jackie Chan [A:82; D:241; M:48, 60], elaborate fight scripting [B:xiii, 5, 16-17; G:68; K:39; L:93, 95, 103, 107, 135; M:50-51; P:28], evil army in *Enter The Dragon* [D:186].

Speedster "lightning" [A:59; C:212; D:116; G:32; L:25 (coin snatch), 42, 95, 113, 146, 150; M:61. D:186 (eyes and intent used for instant strike)]; "...could make the air pop when he hit." [K:36], "fastest fist in the east" [A:55]; normal film speed [A:39; D:76 (slow motion sequence); K:43-44; L:110], tapped the cobra's head [A:71; G:79], de-venomized but not de-fanged [A:71; D:185; K:105; L:110; P:30].

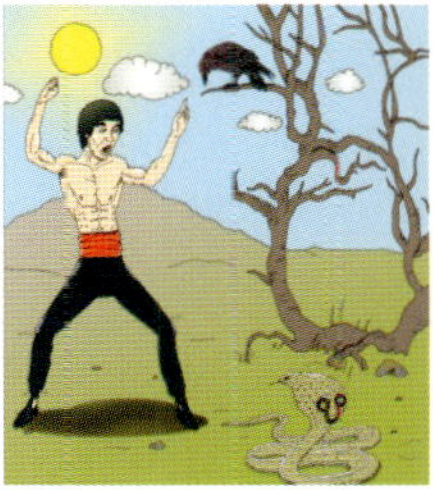

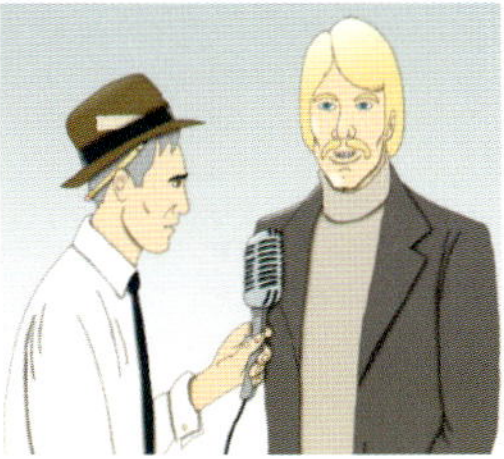

Real Deal utmost respect [L:124]; Chuck Norris [A:60-61; D:278 (Chuck red-faced after sparring); F:148-151; G:64-65, 68, 72; L:90-91, 99, 148-150; M:52-53], "...who would win?" [M:56].

Alpha Male dominated spotlight [L:8], constant flow of lessons, jokes, and bragging [D:112 (entertainer), 217 (show off muscles); L:157; M:54], "trademark" greeting was a snapping kick to the head that just skimmed the nose [D:171; P:30], Ed Parker [A:37; M:19], Jim Kelly: "he can back up his bullshit!" [L:126; O:145-146].

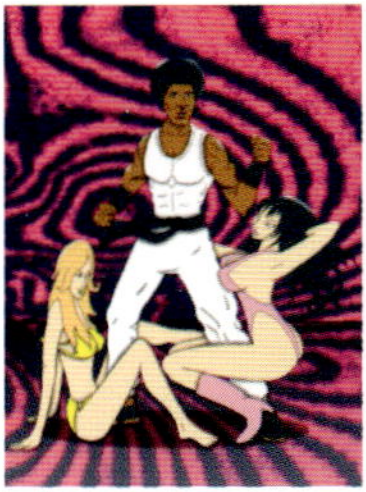

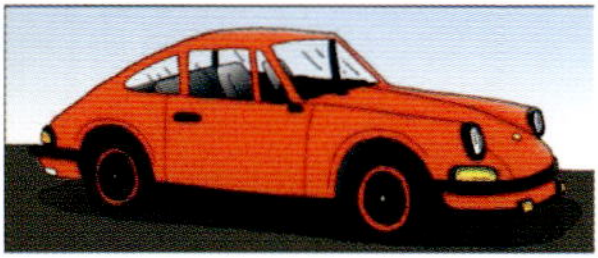

Cruiser blue Chevy Nova [D:76]; red Porsche/Mercedes 350SL/gold Rolls Royce Corniche [D:104, 152, 188; K:84-85; O:139].

Yogi "Meditation and Mental Training" [D:66], meditation [A:64; D:82 (meditate and relax for body and spirit), 206 (enjoyed solitary walks by lake); E:29 ("*I practice gung fu as a ... form of mental training*"); G:xi (focus, centering); O:7], concentrate energy [L:121], cultivated calm to complement explosive potentialities [N:xiv], *"stop all thoughts"* [C 200; E:117], virtue of stretching [G:38; K:84: L:49; M:54; O:77].

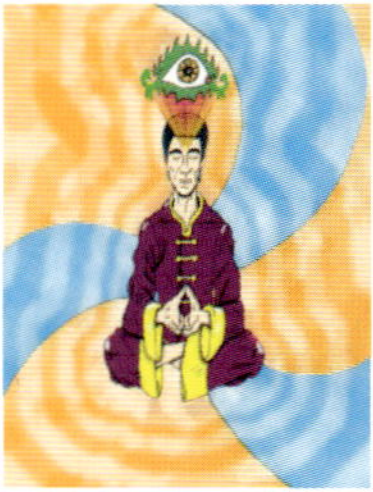

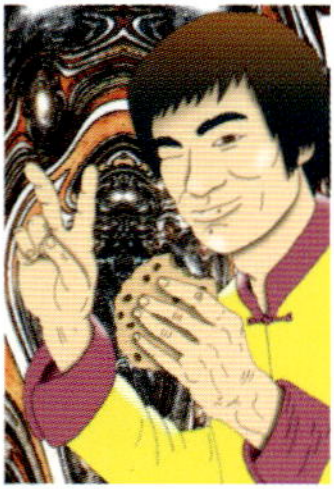

Stoner hash cookies [D:225-226 (Playboy article sparked interest in hash cookies); M:64, 66], chewed cannabis leaf [K:113], no smokes [K:83; L:70; O:152], became "mellow, relaxed, charming" after ingesting [D:225-226 (claimed to buy best quality)], "*time slow down for a little while*" [D:227], peace sign flash [N:73], autopsy results [D:208 (traces in stomach); K:125].

Endurer obsession to make *"fuckingest action motion picture..."* [E:178; O:125; D:191 (pressure to succeed)], dangerous injuries [A:54, 74-75; D:125, 128, 147, 183, 220; E:159; G:79; K:105-106, 121 (serious head blows); L:109], weight-loss [A:53; E:149 ("*I'm down to 128 [pounds]*"); K:75; L 28-29; M:57; O:108, 124], privacy loss [A:58; D:197-199; K:83, 100; L:70; M:57; O:133-134], fight challenges [D:139-140; K:78; O:83-98; P:30], sleeplessness [D:180], nervous facial tic [D:179], amnesia/headaches [D:200], and at least one mysterious seizure [A:76; K:111-113; M:66; P:32-33], sound editing room heat [A:75; D 180, 189; K:111 (heavy, humid Hong Kong summer); P:32].

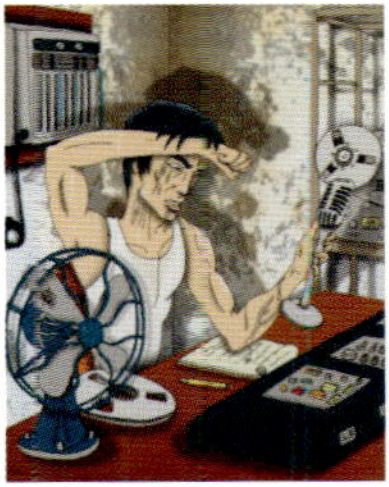

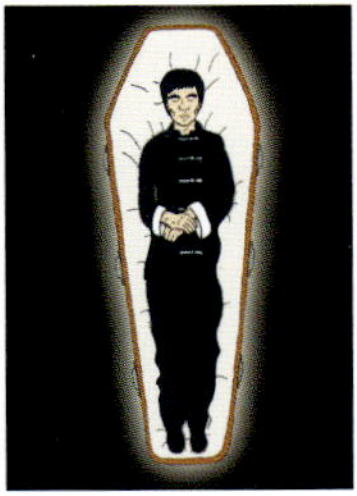

Mortal before big premiere [G:81; M:62-63], lost consciousness [D:203], died at age 32 [B:x; D:xv; K:15; M:62-63; P:37], 1973 [E:17; F:ix, xvii], "death by misadventure" [K:126-129; M:63, 67], cerebral edema or brain swelling from allergic reaction [A:76 (rare); G:95; K:128 (expert testimony about meprobamate and Equagesic); L:31 (five different expert opinions); M:67-68].

Hero post-war statue [Q (Bruce is a "symbol of justice, mastery, and honesty"); R ("one thing we all have in common is Bruce Lee")], poised to pummel [Q (statue in "typical fighting pose"); A:57 ("ready to pounce"); P:16 ("poised to leap")], heroic moral virtue [S].

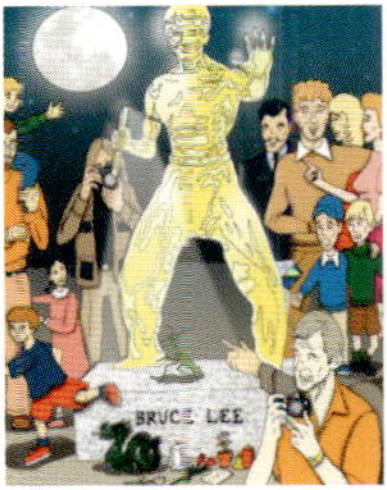

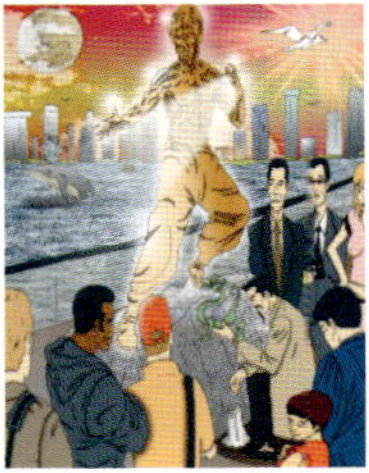

Superstar F:132; K:99; L:131; M:60; enduring [A:8], Hollywood's Walk of Fame [D:255], national hero [D:138; E:153], bronze statue in Hong Kong [D:138].

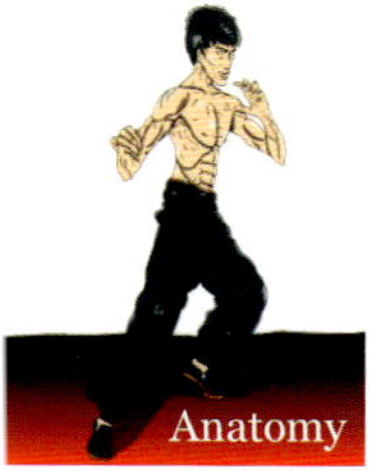

5ft. 7in. [A:7; B:76 (5' 8"); K:31 (5' 7.5"); L:25, 77; M:55; P:14 (little over 5' 7")].

nearsighted [D:8; G:ix].

diet several, austere meals a day [G:38], ginseng [D:64], royal jelly [D:64], rare steak [O:57], protein shake [D:64] vegetable drinks [K:84], cow's blood [O:51], vitamins [D:64], protein powder, banana, ice cream, peanut butter, eggs with shells [O:52].

abs medicine ball [D:64; L:36], leg lifts, sit ups [D:64], electrical stimulus machine [D:250].

knees crawls on knees at his father's funeral [D:71].

back disguised chronic back pain [D:75 (before Green Hornet), 114; E:172 note 6; O:63 (another back injury from a car accident healed by hanging from gravity bar); P:19 (after weightlifting injury)].

genitals rejected from military for undescended testicle physical defect[D:53], circumcised at age 22 [D:52], sired son and daughter [L:8].

isometric presses to summon *chi* [D:64; L:12, 17, 61; O:57], weight train, heavy bag kicks, jog with hand and ankle weights, isometrics, shadow box, skip rope, speed bag, one finger push ups [G:38], hand exercises, leg exercises, running, isometrics, stomach exercises, sparring, free hand exercises [E:105].

forearms nanchaku sticks [D:136-137; L:95-96, 134; O:149, center photos].

"Bruce Three Legs" [D:181];(nicknames celebrating his foot speed also include "Three Kicks Bruce" and "man with three legs" [K:82; O:58].

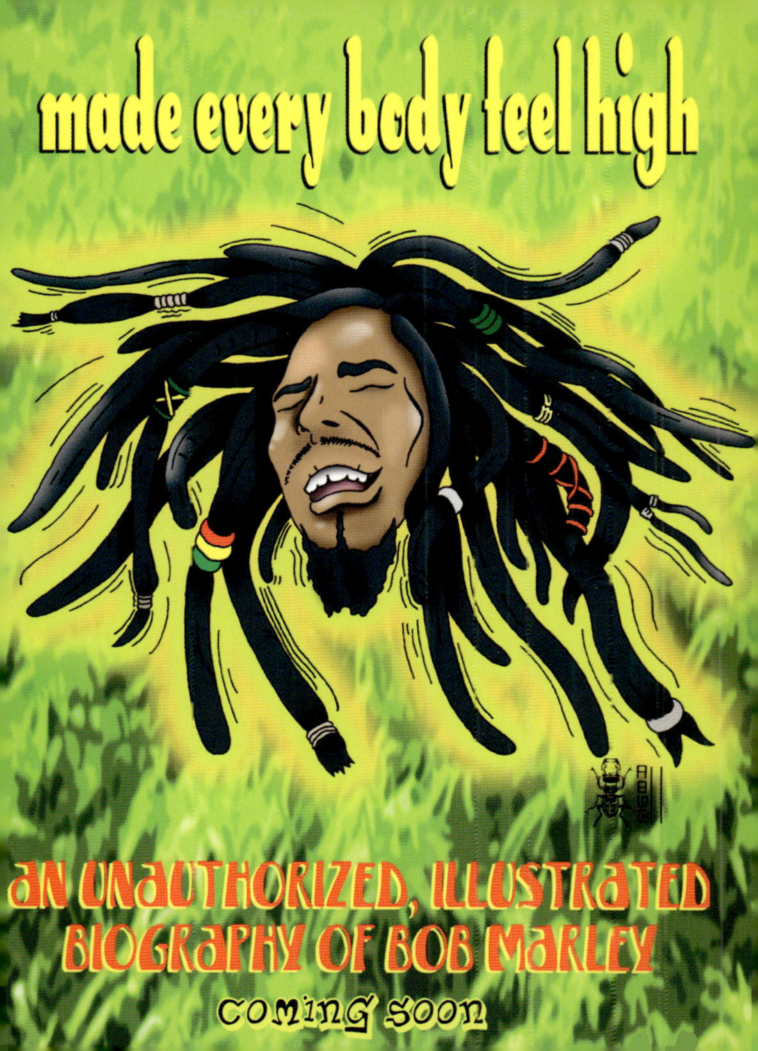
made every body feel high
AN UNAUTHORIZED, ILLUSTRATED BIOGRAPHY OF BOB MARLEY
COMING SOON